Praise
Cultural Sensibility

"Using the concept of cultural sensibility, Sally Ellis Fletcher provides readers with a range of challenging but accessible activities to help them explore their own histories and how their unique culture influences their healthcare provision. Although written for nurses, this book will be invaluable to anyone who wants to understand their perspectives better so that they can deliver excellent care to all patients through mutual understanding, openness, respect, and constructive dialogue."

–Nisha Dogra, PhD, BM, FRPsych
Professor in Psychiatry Education and Honorary
Consultant in Child and Adolescent Psychiatry
Director of MSc in Child and Adolescent Mental Health,
University of Leicester

"Sally Ellis Fletcher does an outstanding job outlining the essentials for a deeper understanding of cultural diversity, inclusivity, and culturally appropriate healthcare. Her sincere approach encourages her audience to think more clearly about the impact of cultural competency—recognizing biases, prejudices, and stereotypes—as it relates to nurses. The discussion questions at the end of each chapter provoke thought and emotion. Cultural Sensibility in Healthcare is a must-read for all patient-centered care providers!"

–Bob Patterson, MSN, RN
President, American Assembly for Men in Nursing
Administrative Director, California Institute for Nursing and Health Care
Doctoral Student, University of San Francisco

CULTURAL SENSIBILITY
IN HEALTHCARE

A Personal & Professional Guidebook

Sally N. Ellis Fletcher, PhD, RN, FNAP

Sigma Theta Tau International
Honor Society of Nursing®

The Honor Society of Nursing, Sigma Theta Tau International (STTI) is a nonprofit organization founded in 1922 whose mission is advancing world health and celebrating nursing excellence in scholarship, leadership, and service. Members include practicing nurses, instructors, researchers, policymakers, entrepreneurs, and others. STTI's 500 chapters are located at more than 675 institutions of higher education throughout Armenia, Australia, Botswana, Brazil, Canada, Colombia, England, Ghana, Hong Kong, Japan, Kenya, Malawi, Mexico, the Netherlands, Pakistan, Portugal, Singapore, South Africa, South Korea, Swaziland, Sweden, Taiwan, Tanzania, Thailand, the United Kingdom, and the United States of America. More information about STTI can be found online at www.nursingsociety.org.

Sigma Theta Tau International
550 West North Street
Indianapolis, IN, USA 46202

To order additional books, buy in bulk, or order for corporate use, contact Nursing Knowledge International at 888.NKI.4YOU (888.654.4968/US and Canada) or +1.317.634.8171 (outside US and Canada).

To request a review copy for course adoption, email solutions@nursingknowledge.org or call 888.NKI.4YOU (888.654.4968/US and Canada) or +1.317.634.8171 (outside US and Canada).

To request author information, or for speaker or other media requests, contact Marketing, Honor Society of Nursing, Sigma Theta Tau International at 888.634.7575 (US and Canada) or +1.317.634.8171 (outside US and Canada).

ISBN: 9781937554958
EPUB ISBN: 9781937554965
PDF ISBN: 9781937554972
MOBI ISBN: 9781937554989

Library of Congress Cataloging-in-Publication Data

Fletcher, Sally N. Ellis, 1954- author.
  Cultural sensibility in healthcare : a personal & professional guidebook / Sally N. Ellis Fletcher.
    p. ; cm.
  ISBN 978-1-937554-95-8 (print : alk. paper) -- ISBN 978-1-937554-96-5 (epub) -- ISBN 978-1-937554-97-2 (pdf) -- ISBN 978-1-937554-98-9 (mobi)
  I. Title.
  [DNLM: 1. Cultural Diversity. 2. Attitude of Health Personnel. 3. Cultural Competency. 4. Delivery of Health Care. WA 31]
  RA427.8
  362.1--dc23
                                        2015014983

First Printing, 2015

PUBLISHER: Dustin Sullivan	**PRINCIPAL BOOK EDITOR:** Carla Hall
ACQUISITIONS EDITOR: Emily Hatch	**DEVELOPMENT EDITOR:** Tonya Maddox Cupp
EDITORIAL COORDINATOR: Paula Jeffers	**COPY EDITOR:** Keith Cline
COVER DESIGNER: Rebecca Batchelor	**PROOFREADER:** Todd Lothery
COVER ILLUSTRATOR: Justine Beckett	**INDEXER:** Jane Palmer
INTERIOR DESIGN: Rebecca Batchelor	

Dedication

This guidebook is dedicated to my amazing family and friends, who supported me in this project. Throughout my career, many persons have honored me by sharing their experiences related to cultural diversity and inclusivity. My heartfelt respect and appreciation are extended to each of you.

Acknowledgments

Special acknowledgment is given to Patricia Chiverton, EdD, RN, FNAP; Mary-Therese Behar Dombeck, PhD, DMin, APRN; Sheldon D. Fields, PhD, ARNP, FNP-BC, AACRN, DPNAP, FAANP; and Jeanne Tuel Grace, PhD, RN, WHNP.

About the Author

Sally N. Ellis Fletcher, PhD, RN, FNAP, is licensed to practice nursing in the states of Kansas, Missouri, and New York. She has taught or served in a clinical capacity in private, public, urban, and rural organizations. Her professional passions are nursing, education, diversity, multiculturalism, entrepreneurship, mentoring, and humanitarianism. She has served on the advisory board for a humanitarian mission trip to Ghana, West Africa, for which she planned and facilitated indigenous and U.S. healthcare providers in delivering healthcare. She is on the board of a local shelter for women and their children who've experienced domestic violence. During her most recent academic tenure, Ellis Fletcher created and designed a program to assist students enrolled in the accelerated education track with socialization, career planning, and cultural inclusiveness in nursing. She also served as co-chair of the Dean's Advisory Council for Cultural Diversity and Inclusiveness and as one of the School of Nursing's faculty diversity officers. Her most recent clinical position was as a clinical nurse researcher who developed the office of Clinical Nurse Research at a Midwestern medical center.

Table of Contents

Foreword

History and circumstances are asking all of us to examine vestiges of the past that continue to plague us today and, at the same time, embrace deeper insights of respectfully being with each other. As we craft impactful responses to the requests, tremendous understanding, a willingness to be vulnerable, and a honing of our due diligence skills will be necessary. This timely book adds further to what we know works and escorts new perspectives and considerations since bias, prejudice, discrimination, and micro and macro aggressions continue to be evident in the caregiving and therapeutic processes.

Moving beyond the rhetoric requires well-defined goals and methodologies for achieving them. Not only do we need to stretch the minds of students and faculty about diversity, we also need to talk about the manifestations of inclusive excellence. Broader than just race, gender, or ethnicity, diversity includes cultural differences such as age, generational differences, socioeconomic status, sexual orientation, religion, body alterations (i.e., tattoos, piercings), body size, disability, marital status, veteran status, professional experience, and educational background. The intersections of all these differences can and often do—in both bold and subtle ways, wearing the bright garments of uniqueness—remind us that all encounters are cultural encounters. Nevertheless, the uniqueness provides the context for care, and this must never be considered as insignificant.

Invisible dynamics related to power and perspective always exist because of people's cultural awareness and proficiency. Making them visible helps to explain the tensions and dynamics encountered when people come together to create solutions for the future. Understanding these concepts and applying the strategies covered in the book chapters can help improve you and the preparation of your students as well as team members—be they faculty or other healthcare providers with their interprofessional experiences. So what and how do we make the spaces in our places of the mind and the physical environment? What good, timely, and wicked questions worthy of answers and why this book was written! Use it for some action-centered pedagogy.

After reading this work, I was reminded of something Nietzsche once said in reference to Diogenes, the Greek philosopher living in the fourth century BC. Before I provide the quote, I should share a bit more about this philosopher. Diogenes now is thought of as an unconventional thinker with a cutting wit and repartee who taught his fellow citizens largely by pantomimic gesture and example. One day, he was reported to have gone about the city in clear daylight with a lit lantern looking about as if he had lost something. When people came up to ask what he was trying to find, he answered: "Even with a lamp in broad daylight, I cannot find a real human being," and when people pointed to themselves, he chased them with a stick shouting, "It is a real human being I want." Bizarre as this may seem, Diogenes' antics did jar the moral consciousness of some, and even now, it nudges us to reflect on the question we are still asking and should always ask: What is the nature of a human being? And what does it mean to ask this question? Now as promised, the Nietzsche quote that came to the forefront of mind was, "Whoever is searching for the human being first must find the lantern." Like Diogenes, Sally Ellis Fletcher's book is a lamp throwing some light on the complexity of how to be culturally relevant. I recommend it for your teaching, curriculum adaptations, and personal growth.

–G. Rumay Alexander, EdD, RN, FAAN
Professor and Director-Office of Multicultural Affairs
University of North Carolina at Chapel Hill School of Nursing

Introduction

If you are interested in cultural inclusiveness, cultural competence, cultural humility, and cultural diversity, I encourage you to continue reading. Using various activities such as journaling, word games, and scenarios, this guidebook asks you to use critical and reflective thinking skills to explore the process of cultural sensibility. What is cultural sensibility? In short, *cultural sensibility* refers to deliberate behaviors that proactively provide an enriched provider–consumer/patient interaction, where the healthcare provider acknowledges cultural issues and situations through thoughtful reasoning, responsiveness, and discreet (attentive, considerate, and observant) interactions.

I was searching for a term that implied practical, applied behaviors, attitudes, and approaches to equip healthcare workers in what is currently discussed as cultural competence, cultural sensitivity, cultural humility, cultural diversity, and various other terms that highlight differences and the grouping of individuals according to their lack of similarity with healthcare workers. These terms are not wrong, negative, or bad, and they have a critical place in the evolving continuum addressing cultural implications in the delivery of healthcare. However, these terms do not equip healthcare workers with skills to address personal issues of bias and stereotypes that can lead to provider-biased healthcare and contribute to healthcare disparities. Drawing from definitions, synonyms, and antonyms in thesauruses and dictionaries, I examined existing cultural terms in search of a word that would emphasize behaviors and attitudes when combined with the word *culture*. The best term was *sensibility*, which describes a responsiveness of both the conscious and emotional senses. From this review, the definition of cultural sensibility was envisioned.

A review of the literature identified an earlier grappling by Dogra (2003) with concepts surrounding cultural diversity. Her work compared two models for teaching cultural diversity: cultural expertise and her term cultural sensibility. Later she used her comparisons to explore medical students' learning about cultural diversity beyond the expertise (categorical) approach of teaching cultural group differences and utilized her concept of cultural sensibility (Dogra & Karnik, 2003). The authors drew clear distinctions between:

- **Cultural expertise:** Proficiency in applying facts

- **Cultural sensitivity:** The degree of compassion and understanding

- **Cultural sensibility:** A broader perspective that implies an action toward openness

Cultural sensibility offers healthcare providers a process that encourages them to first consider their own attitudes, biases, beliefs, and prejudices through self-reflection. The process of self-reflection allows us the opportunity to accept or change our biases, beliefs, and prejudices. Most important, however, it allows us to recognize that these areas have the potential to interfere with effective healthcare interactions.

In each chapter of this guidebook, you have an opportunity to reflect on the actions described in various scenarios and perhaps identify similar experiences from your professional practice. As you do so, you can start to leverage historical experiences to enhance in-the-moment clinical experiences using reflection-in-action (Albanese, 2006) and thus create culturally sensible healthcare encounters.

Target Audience

This guidebook is primarily designed for nurses and pre-licensed nurses who are interested in cultural diversity, inclusivity, and culturally appropriate healthcare. Throughout this guidebook, you are challenged to examine cultural issues beyond just theory and to instead explore culture as it affects your professional role.

Educators might find this guidebook useful as a companion text, one that encourages students to consider practical effects of cultural sensibility in courses where cultural content in healthcare is covered. In addition, schools of nursing with low-diversity faculty/student populations might find this guidebook enlightening, as it prompts readers to consider the healthcare experience from a wider perspective. Likewise, organizations experiencing rapid shifts in their consumer population may find this guidebook an invaluable resource.

Although this guidebook derives from my nursing experience and perspective, most healthcare workers will find the comprehensive examples helpful. Because this guidebook encourages reflection on your life and behaviors, do not hesitate to seek help from your professional support services as you read and participate in the activities if you are dealing with unresolved emotional experiences.

Maya Angelou is credited with saying, "When you know better, you do better." It is my hope that after learning cultural sensibility skills, we will know better, but more important, we will do better.

References

Dogra, N. (2003). Cultural expertise or cultural sensibility? A comparison of two ideal type models to teach cultural diversity to medical students. *International Journal of Medicine, 5*(4), 223–231.

Dogra, N., & Karnik, N. (2003). First-year medical students' attitudes toward diversity and its teaching: An investigation at one U.S. medical school. *Academic Medicine, 78*(11), 1191–1200.

1

CULTURAL SENSIBILITY:
PERSONAL AND
PROFESSIONAL

Consider the following conversation between a young college student (YCS) and the academic dean of a church-related liberal arts college (based on a true experience, but altered here slightly to maintain anonymity):

YCS: Dean, why did you devote your entire life to the church?

Dean: That's a very good question, YCS. I wanted to serve God full time as a minister.

YCS: Oh. Did you always want to be a full-time minister?

Dean: No, I wanted to become an actor and go into the theater like my family.

YCS: Wow, an actor?

Dean: In our family, we were always playing different characters from theater, musicals, television programs, or books. We were constantly acting. We even held our own "Tony Awards."

YCS: An actor. Isn't that an extreme leap from the ministry?

Dean: Perhaps, but for me, life is an enormous opportunity to act. So, I minister full time and act when I'm confronted with the situations of life that are opposite my personal desires. I do what I have to do as a character, like from a play.

YCS: The YCS said nothing else but simply thought, "Gee, that's strange."

I am not a thespian, my family is not theatrical, and as of this writing, I have yet to see a Broadway production. Even so, I am completely fascinated with live theater. However, it is not an essential element of who I am. It is not *my* cultural experience. In the conversation you just read, theater is the cultural experience of the academic dean. The world of theater is intricately woven into the dean's responses and view of the world. We could even surmise that it influences his values, beliefs, communications, and so much more about how he navigates through daily activities.

Unlike the dean, though, many of us are unaware of how cultural influences impact our own actions. This guidebook serves as an antidote to our tendency toward cultural myopia. The focus here is on cultural sensibility in healthcare delivery, and so we'll explore culture from both a *pragmatic* and a *personal* perspective. Let's start with the personal.

Seeing the World From Our Own Perspective

Because much of my work involves examining cultural influences, I often hear, "I don't have a culture." I also hear, "I'm not Jewish," "I'm not Latino," and "I'm not African American." However, these refutations represent a narrow view of what culture is. Remember that culture is more than one's **ethnic group** (*individuals who self-identify membership with or belong to a group with shared values, ancestry, and experiences* [Leininger & McFarland, 2002]).

So, the first step in our cultural sensibility journey is to visit points in our personal history from which we derive meaning, insight, encouragement, and inspiration.

Culture influences how we see the world. It guides and shapes how we think politically, socially, and personally. If we fail to know or recognize our cultural history, we may be disconnected from the reality of why we do the things we do. **Cultural sensibility** (*a deliberate proactive behavior by healthcare providers who examine cultural situations through thoughtful reasoning responsiveness and discreet interactions*) allows us to recognize that we all have a personal history that has been woven together from various experiences and events that guide our life today and that will influence our future. Often, we recall only the positive events that influence our life. In reality, though, both positive and negative experiences build our personal history. As you work through this guidebook, always reference your personal history, especially those events that steered you toward a healthcare career and that may still influence how you respond to cultural issues in healthcare today.

Have you heard of Michael Crichton? The award-winning novelist was perhaps best known for writing *Jurassic Park*. He also wrote *The Andromeda Strain*, in 1969, and created the television series *ER*. His works famously incorporate detailed scientific research that captivates readers. However, few probably know that Mr. Crichton earned a medical degree from Harvard Medical School. Mr. Crichton was actually Dr. Crichton. If you didn't know this about him, you, too, might have wondered how he could incorporate superb scientific detail into his novels. Most likely, the answer is that his personal experiences as a medical student and physician and his passion for science and computers led to that particular skill (Goodreads, 2013; "Michael Crichton: The official site," 2013).

Although few of us will ever gain the recognition and prominence achieved by Michael Crichton, we each have a personal history that influences how we embrace and respond to our healthcare professional role. Our initial desire to pursue a healthcare career, influenced by different motivations/catalysts for each of us, inspired our individual goal/vision to become a healthcare provider. That vision resulted in emotional, mental, and spiritual idealism regarding healthcare. Our idealism allowed us to dream and develop hopes about our future as a healthcare worker.

Because cultural sensibility begins with self-examination, as mentioned earlier, it is time for a few questions:

1. Have you become less open to colleagues and consumers of healthcare services (patients) than when you be-

gan your journey toward becoming a healthcare professional?

Yes ____   No ____

2. Do any of the following issues negatively affect your view of your career as a healthcare provider?

    Use Y for yes and N for no.

    ____ Sociocultural dynamics that diminish trust and your dreams

    ____ Family dynamics (births, marriages, financial challenges, aging parents)

    ____ Powerlessness to reshape your personal vision to fit the needs of today's world

    ____ World events that cause you to become introspective and nostalgic for the safety of the past, with a focus on me and mine

3. Do you feel overwhelmed by the rapid amount of change and information overload that occurs in your personal and professional life?

    Yes ____   No ____

Let's discuss these questions from a general perspective. Our idealism and initial vision of our future in healthcare may no longer guide us today (question 1). If that's so, it certainly cannot provide inspiration for tomorrow. If this describes you, how did that happen? Perhaps you have lost the drive that initially led you to a healthcare career. Again, why?

Our lives change over the years based on any number of factors, including those listed in question 2. Perhaps you've been a healthcare provider for only a relatively short time, though, and none of the factors listed in that question apply to you. Even so, maybe you're experiencing 21st century rapid change and information overload (question 3). After all, our email inboxes are chock-full of information daily (sometimes hourly), and you might find such a rapid pace of information overload overwhelming. Maybe you create task lists that you end up continually adding to as more information (instructions/orders) becomes available (and therefore you can never quite complete the task list).

AUTHOR'S NOTE

Farrell (2013) holds that email is an outdated communication method. It is too slow and too singular in its reach. So, we turn to Facebook, Twitter, and other social media. Those other platforms enable us to share (both send and receive) information with wider audiences more rapidly. Within 5 to 10 years, though, the popular social media of today will likely be replaced by newer technologies that more appropriately meet our future requirements.

Maybe our past, present, and imagined future come into conflict today, diminishing the once wide-eyed idealism of a new healthcare professional. Think carefully about these issues; they have a profound impact both personally and professionally. After all, when we lose our idealism and career goals/vision, we risk being physically present at work but professionally absent in our career as a healthcare provider.

Becoming a Healthcare Provider: A Timeline of Influences

To recapture a bit of our idealism and the vision we had for our healthcare career, let's use a timeline technique to explore what led us to healthcare when we were still "starry-eyed" and the vision for our career in healthcare was vibrant.

Author's Note: If factors that led you into healthcare involve traumatic experiences, you might want to just glance through this section, especially if you have not fully emotionally healed from those events. You are also encouraged to seek professional assistance through an employee assistance program or personal counselor if you find this timeline activity emotionally disturbing.

Let's begin by examining the life event timelines of two nurses. The information presented in the timelines was collected by asking each person to share why she selected nursing as a career and what kept her interested in nursing throughout the years.

Welcome's Timeline

1919	Welcome is born to Bill and Arizona.
	She was raised in a close-knit community in a Midwestern town in the United States.
	Her father was a World War I veteran who worked odd jobs after the war and became a fireman, working the required 24-hour shifts at the town fire station.
	Her mother worked odd jobs and was a housewife.
1925	Arizona (Welcome's mother) dies after a ruptured appendix. Welcome is 6 years old at the time.
	Bill cherishes Welcome and teaches her self-reliance and respect for others.
1929	Bill marries Nila, a schoolteacher, who rules with firmness and a loving heart. Besides teaching, Nila is very involved in the community. Welcome is 10 years old.

1931	Almost every year, after the snow melts, a fire breaks out at the paper mill (as do other fires in other places throughout the year). Whenever disasters strike in the community, Nila and Welcome cook food to take to the disaster site for workers, families, and the injured.
1933	Bill is injured in a paper mill fire and hospitalized. Mr. Jaspers, a fellow fireman and family friend, also is injured. Welcome describes him as being very swollen and puffy when she arrives at the hospital to visit. Welcome is in the hospital room visiting both men when Mr. Jaspers dies. She is distraught and fears that her father will swell and die (a common occurrence with injured firefighters). Welcome is comforted and supported by the Catholic nuns who are nurses. Welcome is 14 years old. Her father recovers.
1936	Welcome graduates from high school at 17 years old. She wants to go to New York and design clothes, but Bill and Nila encourage her to seek a career that will provide greater independence and stability.
1938	Welcome remembers how much she enjoyed helping out after disasters, her fascination with hospitals, and how impressed she was with the nuns who were nurses. She knew of several nurses in the community who graduated nursing school from General Hospital #2 in the state of Missouri.

Welcome applies and is accepted to begin nurse training at General Hospital #2 in Kansas City, Missouri. Welcome is 19 years old. |
| 1941 | Welcome completes nurse training and becomes an RN. |
| 1946 | Now married to a physician, Welcome and her husband work at the city hospital. She also teaches student nurses and, serving as a supervisor, responds to a large number of the emergencies in the hospital. |

1955	Welcome completes her bachelor's degree in nursing from the local Catholic college.
	She enjoys teaching students, has a deep sense of compassion for people, and is still fascinated with hospitals.
	Nursing provides the independence and flexibility Welcome seeks as she raises their children.
	Though often encouraged to stop working and be financially supported by her husband, Welcome enjoys the economic security nursing provides.
1960	She begins working as a school nurse.
1962	She earns a master's degree in teaching.
1970	Welcome continues working as a public school nurse and part-time at the local pediatric hospital.
1981	She retires from full-time nursing.
2013	Though retired for 32 years, Welcome continues to use public health nursing principles daily, regardless of the setting.
	She states that she is still fascinated with aspects of healthcare and has a deep compassion for people.

Discussion question: Can you identify where Welcome was idealistic/vulnerable in her nursing life? What situations would have caused her to exhibit empathy and open up emotionally as a caregiver?

_____

_____

_____

_____

Discussion question: List five influences on Welcome's life that might inform her cultural sensibility.

_____

_____

_____

_____

Discussion question: Is it important that we do not know Welcome's race or cultural background?

_____

_____

_____

_____

The following facts and experiences (among others) might affect how Welcome perceives different cultures:

- Being born in the United States (specifically in the Midwest)
- Having the parents she had
- Seeing someone suffer fatal burns
- Losing her mother young
- Being helped by Catholic nuns
- Being married to a doctor
- Completing higher education

As Welcome reminisced about why she went into nursing (and stayed), she identified several themes that were interwoven throughout her life. These themes were independence, experience, and involvement with disasters. Another theme was the inspiration from the Catholic nuns as they responded to healthcare issues in the community. Welcome is quick to tell you that she experienced some difficult periods as a nurse. In retrospect, though, she reflects on the positive influences and states that she loves nursing and healthcare. (Yes, if you did your math, Welcome was 94 years old when I interviewed her.)

Let's explore a second timeline, this time for Mary.

Mary's Timeline

1955	Mary is born in the northern Midwest part of the United States to loving parents.
	She recalls a deep fascination with human behaviors.
1968	Throughout her childhood, an aunt suffered with mental illness, and other family members exhibited behavioral issues.
	As a child, she enjoys playing school, with her always in the role of the teacher. She creates classrooms with boxes and teaches her toys and sometimes her playmates.
1972	As a member of church and youth groups, Mary visits nursing homes and assists members in the community. This experience provides an exposure to community healthcare for Mary.
1973	Mary is the first generation in her family to attend college.
	While visiting with the high school career counselor, she notices a brochure on mental healthcare providers. A program is being offered through the community college. She decides to enroll in the program.

1975	Mary earns an associate of science degree with an emphasis in mental healthcare.
	She begins working as a mental healthcare technician (MHT) in a hospital.
	Mary's fascination with human behavior continues as she enjoys her job as an MHT.
	Mary is surrounded by RNs and decides she could do what they do as mental healthcare nurses.
	Mary makes plans to return to school.
	Mary marries her longtime boyfriend.
1982	She earns a bachelor of science degree in nursing.
	She dislikes the rigidity of hospital structure.
1983	Mary's first child is born.
	She enjoys working on the eating disorder unit.
1985	She seeks nursing positions that allow teamwork, autonomy, and working with human behavior.
	Mary is recruited to begin teaching in the associate degree nursing program at a community college.
1987	She begins work toward a master's degree in mental health nursing.
	She enjoys teaching because it provides autonomy, teamwork, and the joy of seeing nursing through the eyes of students entering the profession.
1991	Mary completes her master's degree in mental health nursing.
1993	She begins working at a 4-year college in a baccalaureate nursing program.
2006	Mary becomes department director of the nursing program.

	She continues to enjoy autonomy, teamwork, and seeing nursing through the eyes of students entering the profession.
2012	Mary retires from the position of department director of the nursing program. She takes on a consultant role to schools of nursing.

Discussion question: Where was Mary idealistic/vulnerable in her nursing life? What situations would have caused her to exhibit empathy and open up emotionally as a caregiver?

_____

_____

_____

_____

Discussion question: List five influences on Mary's life that might inform her cultural sensibility.

_____

_____

_____

_____

Discussion question: Is it important that we do not know Mary's race or cultural background?

_____

_____

_____

_____

The following facts and experiences, as well as others, might affect how Mary perceives different cultures:

- Having mental illness in her family
- Being a church member
- Being attracted to teaching and human behavior
- Being the first in her family to attend college
- Having children

During our conversation, Mary emphasized multiple times that there was no grand plan to her becoming a nurse and a nurse educator; it just evolved. The following themes were interwoven throughout her life: fascination with the behavior of people, her love for teaching, and a need for autonomy and flexibility.

The Power of One (Or Two, in This Case)

According to the Bureau of Labor Statistics (2012), there were 2,737,400 registered nurses employed in the United States in 2010. The American Nurses Association (2011) identifies 3.1 million licensed registered nurses in the United States. That's a lot of nurses! Yet, I believe in the power of one. Welcome and Mary represent the power of one. They have touched countless lives throughout their careers. I'm sure that there were moments when they had bad days or forgot their reasons for entering healthcare. However, they were still able to draw on their original motivations/catalysts for becoming a healthcare provider. Even Welcome, whose RN license is no longer active, can be heard saying to staff in her independent senior living center, "Would you mind checking on George; he might be dehydrated," or, "His shirt is on wrong, and he is not responding as quickly to questions," or, "It's about flu season, and so it's time to have our hand-washing reminders." Generally, her assessments are accurate, and one might say that for Welcome, "Once a nurse, always a nurse."

Welcome's and Mary's timelines allowed us to explore the motivations/catalysts and themes that were interwoven throughout their lives. Similarly, we each have these ourselves (as you'll explore in the following section), and they represent the essence of our decision to enter into and remain in a healthcare career.

Activity: Build Your Own Timeline

Now it's your turn. Reflect on the experiences in your life that led you to a career in healthcare. Use pen and paper, your word processor, or your tablet to respond to the following questions. It's okay to write your responses in incomplete sentences. Content is important here, not form.

1. Why did you select nursing as a career? Try to recall the earliest motivations possible. Don't hesitate to call your parents or siblings and ask them what they recall as your earliest interest in healthcare.

   _____

   _____

   _____

   _____

2. What has kept you interested in nursing throughout the years?

   _____

   _____

   _____

   _____

3. Create your personal timeline of influences. Refer to Welcome's and Mary's timelines for help.

- Enter your name above the blank timeline.

- Review the information you recorded in steps 1 and 2. If you recall additional events that are important, great. Include them.

- Organize the information according to year.

Timeline of Influences:
(Your Name Goes Here)

4. Review your timeline.

   • What themes are interwoven throughout your life?

   • What additional information should you add?

Discussion question: At what periods were you idealistic/vulnerable in your nursing life? What situations would have caused you to exhibit empathy and open up emotionally as a caregiver?

_____

_____

_____

_____

Discussion question: List five influences from your timeline that might inform your cultural sensibility.

_____

_____

_____

_____

The themes identified from your personal timeline should provide you with encouragement, pride, and an overall "positive energy deposit" into your professional healthcare career today. Your timeline is a reminder of the milestones that have shaped your views and how you respond to patients in your daily practice of healthcare. Likewise, the patients we serve have experienced milestones that influence how they respond to wellness, illness, healthcare providers, and the healthcare system. The milestones on their timelines, just like ours, make them who they are. If we look at each other through the lens of one's timeline, we might better understand the actions, reactions, and viewpoints of others.

Keeping Control of Distractors

Now that we've explored personal timelines and why we selected healthcare as a profession, let's discuss challenges in healthcare that may interfere with or even block our cultural sensibility. Consider the conversion from paper charts to electronic health records (EHRs), text messaging, and mobile phones that place direct-care providers in constant communication with all members of the healthcare system while trying to provide direct patient care. Can you think of other challenges?

The Constant Nature of Change

The demands and changes prompted by technology like converting to EHR can be a steep learning curve with major financial implications for most U.S. healthcare systems. Yet some organizations have made or are making the transition with fewer "hiccups" than others. How can that be? One answer may be in how an organization views change. In 1970, Alvin Toffler, a futurist, published a controversial book, *Future Shock*. In it, he described a future where technology controlled our lives and we were bombarded with so much information we experienced the phenomenon he termed *information overload*. Though countless disagreed with many of the futuristic predictions outlined in the book, Toffler's basic premise regarding an overloaded feeling from excessive information generated by technology was correct. In most of our daily routines, we stop to view Facebook, tweets, emails, instant messaging, and various other posts on our portable technological devices. Many of us review work-related electronic communications during weekends, holidays, and even vacations (all so that we're not behind when we return to work). However, if an organization embodies the primary premise from Toffler's book, "Change is not merely necessary to life—it is life" (Goodreads, 2013), that organization may be more nimble, open, and responsive to change. An organization like that has learned from history and creates processes allowing its workforce to not only adapt to rapid change but also remain idealistic and visionary about opportunities change affords. Likewise in our personal lives, if we embrace the idea that change will continuously happen, we may be empowered to become more nimble and creatively responsive to change.

Earlier in this chapter, in the section "Seeing the World From Our Own Perspective," you answered three questions about yourself. As you continue to ask yourself these questions, new thoughts and insights should be revealed. A yes or no response is *not* diagnostic. The goal is to expand our self-awareness. Remember that if you are weighed down by social dynamics and family demands, feel powerless toward influencing change, and are overloaded with information, you will not be able to be idealistic, open, energized, or present to provide culturally sensible healthcare.

You can regain or create a vision for today and tomorrow as a healthcare provider by recalling and embracing your personal history, your timeline. Reflecting on the original desire that guided you into healthcare, you can gently begin to embrace yesterday's desire as an energizer for today's needs as a healthcare provider. But this can be scary because it requires us to be open, idealistic/vulnerable and dare to consider someone else's timeline (an empathetic view) and its impact on that person's actions and reactions.

At the core of cultural sensibility is the willingness and empathetic temperament to consider the other person's perspective. I was once told that the Cherokee tribe, as part of a life lesson, taught that it is not good to judge until you walk a mile in the other person's shoes. Seeing life from the perspective of another is a lesson we can never outgrow. It requires us to leave our introspective world and become a risk-taker. As a risk-taker, you must approach in a nonjudgmental way anyone who may appear different from the way you look, think, believe, and act. I don't know about you, but sometimes this is difficult (and downright scary) for me to do. However, I realize it is vital for healthcare providers to recall the Cherokee life lesson and to consider the footsteps that each patient and colleague has taken to arrive at his or her personal viewpoints.

The Power of Many

Number-wise, nursing is a powerful workforce with a large power base that can set the tone for a compassionate, culturally sensitive, and culturally sensible healthcare delivery system. A base this large means that nurses can also set a healthcare tone that is apathetic, disillusioned, and alienated from the essence of good healthcare delivery. When our interactions with patients/colleagues lack cultural sensibility, we become less effective and less able to bring hope, healing, and inspiration to those who seek our services as healthcare providers. Therefore, let's reexamine our primary motivations for selecting healthcare as a career.

I will go out on a limb and say that most healthcare providers experienced no lightning strikes, angels with harps, or dreams or visions that told us to make healthcare our career. For some, it was a deliberate and calculated career choice, minus the theatrics or cinematography. Most of us were guided by circumstances, life events and desires, opportunities, and our belief that a career in healthcare would provide (at least some) personal enjoyment. But when was the last time we revisited the catalysts that launched us on our professional healthcare journey? Our motivations/catalysts differ for each of us, but we can all benefit from revisiting the events that led us into healthcare.

Before finishing this section, let's explore the number of nurses in the U.S. Based on national employment projections, registered nurses rank number 5 among the largest employment occupations in the United States (CareerOneStop, 2013). If you're curious (as I was), you may wonder what other occupations were identified. So, I've listed CareerOneStop's top 10 occupations.

#	Occupation	Employ-ment 2012	Typical Education
1	Retail salespeople	4,447,000	Less than high school
2	Cashiers	3,338,900	Less than high school
3	Office clerks, general	2,983,500	High school diploma or equivalent
4	Combined food preparation and serving workers, including fast food	2,969,300	Less than high school
5	Registered nurses	2,711,500	Associate's degree
6	Customer service representatives	2,362,800	High school diploma or equivalent
7	Waiters and waitresses	2,362,200	Less than high school
8	Secretaries and administrative assistants, except legal, medical, and executive	2,324,400	High school diploma or equivalent
9	Janitors and cleaners, except maids and housekeeping cleaners	2,324,000	Less than high school
10	Laborers and freight, stock, and material movers, hand	2,197,300	Less than high school

The next healthcare occupation after nursing in 2012 is listed at number 17 (nursing assistants); physicians didn't make it into the top 50. Additional healthcare provider occupations are listed in the following table.

#	Occupation	Employ-ment 2012	Typical Education
17	Nursing assistants	1,479,800	Postsecondary nondegree award
25	Personal care aides	1,190,600	Less than high school
35	Home health aides	875,100	Less than high school
41	Licensed practical and licensed vocational nurses	738,400	Postsecondary nondegree award

Categorical Knowledge Limitations

Part of what prompted my journey to cultural sensibility was my personal frustration with healthcare providers wanting lists for each ethnic or racial group that presents to their respective agency. Essentially, providers were requesting categorical lists for *every* group: an impossible task.

Categorical knowledge as it relates to culture describes information about particular racial or ethnic groups that is clustered under headings such as language, food preferences, homeland of origin, religion, and so on. The information provided by categorical knowledge of culture in healthcare is useful and important, but can be misleading. It is impossible to be familiar with all cultures, subcultures, and groups one may encounter, regardless of the way in which the categorical knowledge is presented and learned. If we are not careful, categorical knowledge can limit our perspective and approach toward cultural issues and can increase the risk of stereotyping during consumer/patient interactions. If stereotyping is increased from categorical knowledge, we magnify provider-bias healthcare encounters. If we equip ourselves and other healthcare providers only with categorical knowledge, we may create unnecessary stress, demands, and expectations on healthcare providers when unanticipated cultural groups present to their healthcare practice.

As a healthcare provider, you might recall situations where you scrambled and searched for information that described a cultural group an individual represented, only to then fumble with cultural errors. Confusion and frustration from such attempts to provide culturally appropriate healthcare may restrain future efforts or produce a lackadaisical attitude toward the subject of cultural diversity in healthcare. Consequently, approaching culture in healthcare primarily from the level of categorical knowledge perpetuates culture in healthcare at the intellectual level and may inhibit opportunities to genuinely care for, treat, and respect individuals seeking healthcare based on their culturally unique attributes.

Cultural Sensibility Benefits

Cultural sensibility describes a proactive response, which implies that one is energetic, enthusiastic, and in a state of readiness and openness for some event, occurrence, or phenomenon. It is a deliberate behavior that incorporates systematic and thoughtful reasoning and responsiveness to an event, occurrence, or phenomenon. Sometimes when we are proactive and deliberate, we become overzealous. However, cultural sensibility is not overbearing or bullish. In contrast, it embraces a discreet (attentive, considerate, and observant) behavior during interactions. To move toward a behavioral level of addressing the needs of culture in healthcare, a new process is needed. Cultural sensibility is proposed as one process to move healthcare providers to the level of behavioral cultural sensitivity.

Cultural sensibility offers healthcare providers a process that encourages examination of their attitudes, biases, beliefs, and prejudices through self-reflection. The process of self-reflection allows us the opportunity to accept or change our biases, beliefs, and prejudices. Most important, though, it allows us to recognize that these areas have the potential to interfere with effective healthcare interactions.

Kathryn Stockett wrote in the historical novel *The Help* (2009), "All my life I'd been told what to believe about politics, coloreds, being a girl. But with Constantine's thumb pressed in my hand, I realized I actually had a choice in what I could believe." As healthcare providers, we have a choice in what we believe about patients who seek our healing care. We can incorporate the stereotypes and labels of noncompliant, frequent flyer, drug seeker, and so forth, or we can exhale and examine our attitudes, biases, and beliefs and reflect on what the patients are saying they need from us as healthcare providers.

REALITY CHECK MOMENT

For emergency responders, critical care providers, and other emergency situations, I am not advocating that emergency care be paused for a self-reflection cultural sensibility assessment. As you engage in more and more cultural sensibility interactions, though, they will become second nature, as your previous interactions inform your future ones.

Activity: Consider Whether Healthcare Is a Right or a Privilege

Don't panic, you're not about to read a philosophical, political, sociocultural discussion or debate on the topic of whether healthcare is a right or privilege. If you are a healthcare provider or student enrolled in a healthcare program, you've more than likely already answered this question. If you've recited the Florence Nightingale Pledge or reviewed the Code of Ethics for Nurses or oaths and codes of ethics for your respective healthcare profession, you have considered this question already.

1. If you are a registered nurse, review the Code of Ethics for Nurses and the Nightingale Pledge. If you are a member of another healthcare profession, review your professional code of ethics and any oath that members of your profession recite.

THE NIGHTINGALE PLEDGE

The Florence Nightingale Pledge was modified from the Hippocratic Oath by Lystra E. Gretter in 1893. Since 1893, the pledge has been updated and modified several times. The original version reflects nursing in 1893 and reads as follows:

"I solemnly pledge myself before God and in the presence of this assembly, to pass my life in purity and to practice my profession faithfully. I will abstain from whatever is deleterious and mischievous, and will not take or knowingly administer any harmful drug. I will do all in my power to maintain and elevate the standard of my profession, and will hold in confidence all personal matters committed to my keeping and all family affairs coming to my knowledge in the practice of my calling. With loyalty will I endeavor to aid the physician in his work, and devote myself to the welfare of those committed to my care" (American Nurses Association, 2013).

CODE OF ETHICS FOR NURSES

The Code of Ethics for Nurses (American Nurses Association, 2015) has nine provisions that guide the profession of nursing in its professional responsibilities and conduct:

1. The nurse practices with compassion and respect for the inherent dignity, worth, and unique attributes of every person.

2. The nurse's primary commitment is to the patient, whether an individual, family, group or community, or population.

3. The nurse promotes, advocates for, and protects the rights, health, and safety of the patient.

4. The nurse has authority, accountability, and responsibility for nursing practice; makes decisions; and takes action consistent with the obligation to promote health and to provide optimal care.

5. The nurse owes the same duties to self as to others, including the responsibility to promote health and safety, preserve wholeness of character and integrity, maintain competence, and continue personal and professional growth.

6. The nurse, through individual and collective effort, establishes, maintains, and improves the ethical environment of the work setting and conditions of employment that are conducive to safe, quality healthcare.

7. The nurse, in all roles and settings, advances the profession through research and scholarly inquiry, professional standards development, and the generation of both nursing and health policy.

8. The nurse collaborates with other health professionals and the public to protect human rights, promote health diplomacy, and reduce health disparities.

9. The profession of nursing, collectively through its professional organizations, must articulate nursing values, maintain the integrity of the profession, and integrate principles of social justice into nursing and health policy.

2. Describe how the Code of Ethics and the Nightingale Pledge, or similar documents that represent your profession, answer the question of whether healthcare is a right or a privilege.

_____

_____

_____

_____

3.   Analyze how your personal beliefs impact your practice.

If you wrote that healthcare is a **privilege,** describe how that concept might motivate your state of readiness and openness with patients you encounter.

_____

_____

_____

_____

If you wrote that healthcare is a **right,** describe how that concept might motivate your state of readiness and openness with patients you encounter.

_____

_____

_____

_____

Activity: Consider Your Own Cultural Sensibility

On any given day, healthcare workers face a number of tasks, responsibilities, unexpected changes, and life-and-death situations. Providing culturally appropriate care may seem low on the priority list of urgent tasks to accomplish, especially if one's perspective is "we're all the same."

Read the following scenario.

Two healthcare workers from different ethnic and cultural backgrounds are friends at work and sometimes socialize outside the work environment. On break, Donna tells Maria, "I don't understand this culture stuff. We're all people! Why do we have to make a big deal of everything?"

1. Describe your initial, unfiltered response to Donna.

   _____

   _____

   _____

   _____

2. Have you ever felt like Donna?

   If yes, write why you felt like the comment Donna expressed.

   If no, can you imagine why Donna might feel this way?

   _____

   _____

   _____

   _____

Summary

Cultural sensibility was introduced in this chapter, but the focus was on the healthcare provider. As healthcare providers, we're confronted with so many issues that it's easy to forget that we are the *essence* of healthcare. We are powerful and important and limited only by our belief in that fact. We need energy deposits into our energy accounts to effectively provide healthcare, and one way to renew our enthusiasm/energy is to revisit the motivations/catalysts that directed us toward a career in healthcare. Whether we personally believe healthcare is a right or a privilege, as healthcare providers, we are bound by our professional codes of ethics. The Code of Ethics for Nurses, with its interpretive statements, can provide meaning, direction, encouragement, and motivation when we lose direction, or even that extra boost of emotional energy.

References

American Nurses Association. (2011). American Nurses Association fact sheet: Registered nurses in the U.S. nursing by the numbers. Retrieved from http://nursingworld.org/Content/NNW-Archive/NationalNursesWeek/MediaKit/NursingbytheNumbers.pdf

American Nurses Association. (2013). Florence Nightingale Pledge. Retrieved from http://nursingworld.org/FunctionalMenuCategories/AboutANA/WhereWeComeFrom/FlorenceNightingalePledge.aspx

American Nurses Association. (2015). *Code of Ethics for Nurses: With interpretive statements*. Silver Spring, MD: Author.

Bureau of Labor Statistics, U.S. Department of Labor. Occupational outlook handbook, 2012-13 edition, registered nurses. Retrieved from http://www.bls.gov/ooh/healthcare/registered-nurses.htm

CareerOneStop (2013). Occupations with the largest employment. Retrieved from http://www.careerinfonet.org/oview3. next=oview3&level=overall&optstatus=101000000&id=1&nodeid=5&soccode=&stfips=00&jobfam=&group=1&showall=no

Goodreads (2013). Michael Crichton. Retrieved from http://www.goodreads.com/quotes/tag/history

Farrell, M. (2013, March 30). E-mail a thing of past for business, young. *The Boston Globe*. Retrieved from http://www.bostonglobe.com/business/2013/03/29/mail-gets-cold-shoulder/xWOVx0s9h8EXVs8t6MxrmO/story.html

Michael Crichton: The official site (2013). Retrieved from http://www.michaelcrichton.net/aboutmichaelcrichton-biography.html

Toffler, A. (1970). *Future Shock*. New York, NY: Bantam Books.

Wall, B. M. (2002). The pin-striped habit: Balancing charity and business in Catholic hospitals 1865–1915. *Nursing Research, 51*(1), 50–58.

2

COMMON GROUND:
TERMS AND DEFINITIONS

Communication is one of the most fundamental skills we learn as humans. Through communication, we can share breakthroughs in scientific discoveries, tell people we love them, and enter the world of poetry and great novels. However, *effective* communication is a difficult skill to master, even among family, friends, and similar groups. During communication processes, words selected by either communicator may lack mutual meaning. This can hinder the opportunity for effective communication and may instead produce an unclear communication process and in some instances damage or destroy relationships.

When we add diverse cultural and subcultural meanings to words, the complexity of achieving effective communication becomes more challenging and requires enhanced skills. Glossaries are generally presented as a concluding chapter or appendix of a book. For this guidebook, though, to present a common foundation and enhance communication, this chapter defines carefully selected terms based on their relevance to the discussion of cultural sensibility.

Teenage Communication

Typically, adolescents create and use words with different meanings for their specific purpose during a specific time period. Consider the word *good*. Its meaning conveys something positive, beneficial, or excellent. Over the past 30 years, adolescents in the United States have attached the meaning of the word *good* to words other than the good. Around the 1980s, some adolescents substituted the word *bad* for good. In fact, a fast-food chicken advertisement had a group of young men playing in a band with a gentleman that appeared to be in his 70s. An attractive woman enters announcing that food is here and that it's time to eat the new fast-food chicken recipe. The next scene has the younger men stating, "This new chicken recipe is bad." The camera goes in for a close-up of the older gentleman, who looks puzzled and then replies, "I don't know what you're talking about; this is good chicken!"

In the 1990s, teens could be heard saying "that's the bomb," also conveying to their peer group that something is good. During the early 2000s, "that's dope" implied something was positively good. In most standard dictionaries, *bad, bomb,* and *dope* do not imply something positive, beneficial, or excellent. To a specific subculture of adolescents during specific periods in time, however, the words *bad, bomb*, and *dope* communicated their meaning for the word *good*. To this adolescent subgroup, their use of these words conveyed one meaning, but to outsiders, their conversations would be viewed as confusing and more than likely misinterpreted, as in the chicken commercial. So that we're current with 2015 pop culture, I asked my favorite 19-year-old play niece, Ms. M. P., what current words mean *good* in teen pop culture. She did not disappoint. The following are the current words:

- Sick

- Wicked

- Beast

- Boss (revived from the 20th century)

The fascinating thing about this list is that the usage and meaning will vary according to geography, socioeconomic group, and subculture. I have a question for you: *Are we wicked?*

Fumble: Trying to Score a Communication Touchdown

Communication mishaps occur daily within and between similar as well as different cultural groups. Examples of using words inappropriately between cultures are documented on the Learn English Organization (2013) website "English Horror Mistakes." One example on their site describes a well-known carbonated beverage company that launched its famous slogan in another country, but with an inaccurate translation. The company wanted to say "come alive with the _ _ generation"; instead, it implied that its drink would "raise their loved ones from the dead."

Even in healthcare settings, we've fumbled during communication processes as we've attempted to communicate with patients. Some reading this guidebook may recall that the acronym SOB was once freely used in charts and even when communicating with patients. To healthcare providers, it referred to "shortness of breath." To consumers unfamiliar with the healthcare acronym, we were calling them or their loved one a "son of a b_ _ch." Imagine, or remember, the confusion this created! Here's another example. Do you recall the healthcare acronym PROM? In an obstetrics and gynecology setting, PROM indicated "preterm or premature rupture of membranes." In contrast, if written in a nonobstetrical setting, it referred to "passive range of motion." These examples are a small component of why acronyms are discouraged in healthcare documentation. Using words that have the same or similar meaning for all individuals in the communication process is not only an essential element toward achieving effective communication but also imperative to ensure mutual communication occurs regardless of setting or diversity of communicators.

Activity: Listen Closely

Communication occurs all around us. Observe a conversation at work, home, or play. Try to identify whether all communicators are conveying the same meaning for the same words.

1. What words had a different meaning for each communicator?

   _____

   _____

   _____

   _____

2. Were they able to overcome the difference in the meaning of the word? If so, how did they achieve this?

_____

_____

_____

_____

3. Describe the outcome of the communication process.

_____

_____

_____

_____

Reflecting on how we and those around us communicate is an important step not only in the discussion of cultural sensibility but also in being an effective healthcare professional.

Definitions

Glossaries remind me of party appetizers. They help ease potentially awkward moments by providing a common point of conversation. I hope this grouping of words will stimulate discussions about the terms and definitions provided. It is also my intent that these definitions will provide a common point or a foundation for conversations that surround cultural sensibility. The glossary is not designed to trace the history and meaning of the words presented. By using your favorite search engine, you can find multiple terms with references defining words surrounding culturally appropriate and culturally sensitive healthcare. Though some terms are presented in an annotated format, an exhaustive list of terms and word origins is not provided. (All websites cited are current at the time of this writing.)

Culture

To me, culture is simply the way we do the things we do. In contrast, there are many definitions for the word culture. The following definition is broad, yet specific to healthcare providers and systems.

Culture is:

> The thoughts, communications, actions, customs, beliefs, values, and institutions of racial, ethnic, religious, or social groups. Culture defines how: health care information is received; how rights and protections are exercised; what is considered to be a health problem; how symptoms and concerns about the problem are expressed; who should provide treatment for the problem; and what type of treatment should be given (U.S. Department of Health & Human Services, Office of Minority Health, 2013).

Culturally Appropriate Healthcare

Providing healthcare that is respectful and responsive to the receiver of the healthcare services is my simple definition of the term **culturally appropriate healthcare**. This includes appropriate linguistics. This definition was adapted from the National Standards for Culturally and Linguistically Appropriate Services in Health Care Final Report, Office of Minority Health (2001).

Cultural Bias

The founder of the Transcultural Nursing Society (http://tcns. org), Madeleine M. Leininger, defined **cultural bias** as "a firm position or stance that one's own values and beliefs must govern the situation or decisions" (Leininger & McFarland, 2002, p. 51). When healthcare bias is demonstrated within the healthcare system, at any level or point of entry or encounter, we alienate individuals from seeking healthcare. An example of this is healthcare providers who believe drug addict mothers should not see their babies during the postpartum period.

Cultural Brokering

I think of cultural brokering as a secured bridge that allows individuals with opposing values to walk across with the certainty that the bridge will not sway. "**Cultural brokering** is defined as the act of bridging, linking, or mediating between groups or persons of differing cultural backgrounds for the purpose of reducing conflict or producing change" (Jezewski, 1990).

Cultural Competence

The Office of Minority Health (2013) provides a comprehensive definition of cultural competence adapted from Cross et al.'s seminal 1989 work. It is listed here to expose you to the depth, breadth, and complexity of the term:

> **Cultural and linguistic competence** is a set of congruent behaviors, attitudes, and policies that come together in a system, agency, or among professionals that enables effective work in cross-cultural situations. Culture refers to integrated patterns of human behavior that include the language, thoughts, communications, actions, customs, beliefs, values, and

institutions of racial, ethnic, religious, or social groups. Competence implies having the capacity to function effectively as an individual and an organization within the context of the cultural beliefs, behaviors, and needs presented by consumers and their communities.

The definition further describes cultural competence as an essential resolution in eradicating healthcare disparities. This is a bold statement but rooted in the conviction that culture and language influence both healthcare providers' and patients' beliefs about health, wellness, and illness. They further highlight that culture may influence how a healthcare provider's culture can influence patients' access to healthcare. It is important to note that cultural competence is often discussed as a point of achievement. It is more accurate to view cultural competence as a continuum.

Cultural Clashing

When individuals or groups have opposing cultures (values, beliefs, attitudes, behaviors, norms, and so on) toward a same issue, topic, or activity, this is **cultural clashing**. My visual image of cultural clashing is the amusement park bumper car ride when the cars are all jammed up and none of the cars can move in any direction. This cultural clashing is explored in greater depth in Chapter 3, "Lessening the Impact of Cultural Clashes."

AUTHOR'S NOTE

Throughout this guidebook, you'll see the terms *values, beliefs,* and *norms.* So that the distinction among them is clear, let's briefly define those terms here. Sociologists have produced whole books on the subject, so you've got multiple sources available if you want to learn more about how these terms are used to define a culture. A **value** represents what a culture determines to be desirable or undesirable (good or bad; for example, many cultures value education and hard work). A **belief** is what the culture holds to be true (for example, a particular religion). A **norm** refers to expected behavior that reinforces the culture's values and beliefs (for example, deference to elders). I don't define *behaviors* and *attitudes* here because those are not terms of art, which means that they are generally used in the context of their commonly understood definitions.

Cultural Diversity

The unique difference between groups' values, beliefs, and practices is how I define **cultural diversity**. It is also important to highlight that most healthcare professional organizations provide a cultural diversity definition for their members. In healthcare, nursing is credited with initiating the majority of early work surrounding cultural diversity. Therefore, the 1991 American Nurses Association (ANA) *Position Statement on Cultural Diversity in Nursing Practice* is cited for its broad and historical perspective:

> Cultural diversity in nursing practice derives its conceptual base from nursing, other cross-cultural health disciplines, and the social sciences such as anthropology, sociology and psychology. Culture is conceptualized broadly to encompass the belief systems of a variety of groups. Cultural diversity refers

to the differences between people based on a shared ideology and valued set of beliefs, norms, customs, and meanings evidenced in a way of life. Culture consists of patterns of behavior acquired and transmitted symbols, constituting the distinctive achievement of human groups, including their embodiment in artifacts; the essential core of culture consists of historically derived and selected ideas and especially their attached values (Kroeber & Kluckhohn, 1952).

As of the writing of this guidebook, the ANA has a Diversity Awareness project that you can access at http://nursingworld. org/DiversityAwareness. The project is designed to build on the ANA's Nursing's Social Policy Statement and provide resources that expand diversity awareness for nurses.

Cultural Humility

In 1998, Tervalon and Murray-Garcia addressed the growing concern for cultural competence in medical education with their seminal article that countered the idea of cultural competence as an achievable endpoint and presented cultural humility as a lifelong learning behavior. Their 1998 work continues to be referenced in the 21st century and is the foundation for many cultural initiatives in healthcare. In the article, they describe **cultural humility** as a:

> Process that requires humility as individuals continually engage in self-reflection and self-critique as lifelong learners and reflective practitioners. It is a process that requires humility in how physicians bring into check the power imbalances that exist in the dynamics of physician-patient communication by using patient-focused interviewing and care (p. 118).

Cultural Inclusiveness

Simply put, **cultural inclusiveness** refers to valuing and respecting the contributions that individuals and groups from differing cultures bring to a topic, activity, or institution, with mutual agreement to work through cultural clashes to achieve an inclusive outcome.

CLAS Standards

CLAS stands for **Culturally and Linguistically Appropriate Services**. The initial CLAS Standards were published in 2001 by the U.S. Department of Health & Human Services Office of Minority Health. The purpose of the standards is to inform, guide, and facilitate required and recommended practices related to culturally and linguistically appropriate health services (National Standards for Culturally and Linguistically Appropriate Services in Health Care Final Report, OMH, 2001).

In 2013, the National Standards for Culturally and Linguistically Appropriate Services in Health and Health Care: A Blueprint for Advancing and Sustaining CLAS Policy and Practice was launched to provide broader and more inclusive definitions and applications surrounding culturally and linguistically appropriate services. The definition for **culturally appropriate healthcare** has expanded to services that are respectful of and responsive to individual cultural health beliefs and practices, preferred languages, health literacy levels, and communication needs and employed by all members of an organization (regardless of size) at every point of contact.

The new CLAS Standards comprise 15 standards organized according to the following list:

- Principal Standard (provide effective, equitable, understandable, and respectful quality care and services that are responsive to diverse cultural health beliefs and practices, preferred languages, health literacy, and other communication needs) (1 standard)

- Governance, Leadership, and Workforce (3 standards)

- Communication and Language Assistance (4 standards)

- Engagement, Continuous Improvement, and Accountability (7 standards)

All standards are designed to "advance health equity, improve quality, and help eliminate health care disparities by establishing a blueprint for health and health care organizations" (Office of Minority Health U.S. Department of Health & Human Services, 2013, p. 13).

AUTHOR'S NOTE

A copy of this document is a must-read for individuals and organizations serious about culturally and linguistically appropriate services. It is available at Think Cultural Health, U.S. Department of Health & Human Services, Office of Minority Health.

Cultural Sensibility

I define **cultural sensibility** as a deliberate proactive behavior by healthcare providers who examine cultural situations through thoughtful reasoning, responsiveness, and discreet (attentive, considerate, and observant) interactions. The healthcare provider is aware of his or her preconceived ideas and biases, but strives to separate those personal beliefs from the provider-patient interaction to provide culturally appropriate healthcare.

Cultural Sensitivity

"Understanding the needs and emotions of your own culture and the culture of others" is **cultural sensitivity** (National Center for Cultural Competence, 2004, p. vii). A broader definition for cultural sensitivity is presented by the National Standards for Culturally and Linguistically Appropriate Services in Health Care Final Report, OMH (2001). This definition provides a strong statement that healthcare providers "be appropriately responsive to the attitudes, feelings, or circumstances of groups of people that share a common and distinctive racial, national, religious, linguistic or cultural heritage" (p. 19). Thus, the responsibility for cultural sensitivity is on the healthcare provider, not on the patient.

Ethnic Group

An **ethnic group** consists of individuals who self-identify membership with or belong to a group with shared values, ancestry, and experiences.

Ethnocentrism

Ethnocentrism refers to the belief that one group is superior over others. It can also include viewing different cultural groups from your cultural group's norms, values, and beliefs.

Healthcare Disparities

The U.S. Department of Health & Human Services defines **health disparity** as follows:

> A particular type of health difference that is closely linked with social, economic, and/or environmental disadvantage. Health disparities adversely affect groups of people who have systematically experienced greater obstacles to health based on their racial or ethnic group; religion; socioeconomic status; gender; age; mental health; cognitive, sensory, or physical disability; sexual orientation or gender identity; geographic location; or other characteristics historically linked to discrimination or exclusion (HealthyPeople.gov, 2013).

Nurses should note that in provision 8 of the 2015 Code of Ethics for Nurses that they're to collaborate in "reduce[ing] health disparities."

Race

As a socially constructed category, **race** uses physical characteristics to group peoples. The term race is constructed differently and with different implications around the world.

Reflective Practice

The term **reflective practice** is rooted in the work of Donald Alan Schön (1930–1997), whose premise was that professionals practice predominately in a tacit or "knowing-in-action" categorized framework. The framework is beneficial but can prevent practitioners from recognizing new occurrences (phenomena) that are not related to the knowing-in-action categories. However, practitioners who embrace a reflective practice operate from a reflection-in-action perspective in which they are constantly reflecting, challenging, and evaluating their knowing-in-action processes, in addition to recognizing, reflecting, challenging, and evaluating new occurrences (phenomena). Seminal references for this definition include Albanese, 2006; Epstein, 1999; Mamede & Schidt, 2004; and Schön, 1983.

Reflective practice is presented in this discussion as a means toward achieving a culturally sensible practice. Later scenarios that will be presented are followed by a series of questions. Through the scenarios and questions, you will be exposed to the reflection process and begin to recognize, reflect, challenge, and evaluate not only existing knowing-in-action categories but also new occurrences in your actual clinical practice.

Activity: Apply These Definitions to Your Own Practice

Review the definitions in this chapter, and then answer the following questions:

1. When you provide healthcare, whose perspective are you using to provide the care?

   _____

   _____

2. Do you provide care from a me-centered perspective?

   _____

   _____

3. Do you provide care from an awareness of needs and emotions of the culture of the patients you serve, as well as your own?

_____

_____

4. Do you consider opportunities for cultural clashes (see Chapter 3) and cultural bonding?

_____

_____

Next time you're in your practice setting, think again about these questions and consider to what extent you are achieving cultural sensibility in your provider-patient interactions.

Activity: Document Cultural Differences

1. What do you do every year on December 24?

_____

_____

2. What do you do on the last Monday in May every year?

_____

_____

3. Now individually ask five people who are not your family, social group, workmates, or party buddies the preceding questions. Try to ask people you do not know very well. If you are shy about asking the question, tell them you're completing an assignment. Remember not to share your answers with them until they've responded to both questions. Be sure to ask the questions in an environment that is safe and in which you feel safe interacting with the person. Write their responses in the spaces provided.

- What do you do every year on December 24?

    Person 1: _____

    Person 2: _____

    Person 3: _____

    Person 4: _____

    Person 5: _____

- What do you do on the last Monday in May every year?

    Person 1: _____

    Person 2: _____

    Person 3: _____

    Person 4: _____

    Person 5: _____

Congratulations on completing the activity. First review the answers. Hopefully, your answers are different from the five people you asked. Each question refers to a specific day, and each response conveys a different idea and meaning. Let's look at the questions.

- What do you do every year on December 24? For some, this day is called Christmas Eve.

- What do you do on the last Monday in May every year? For Americans, this day is called Memorial Day.

Now consider if you were involved in a conversation with the same five individuals and you had begun talking about Memorial Day or Christmas Eve. The same words could have a different meaning or, for some, no meaning at all. Words and their meanings are important. As you progress through this guidebook, refer back to this chapter as often as you need to for clarification of these sometimes confusing (and confusingly similar) terms defined throughout this chapter.

Power Differential: The Power of Healthcare Providers

An aspect or concept that is important to the discussion of cultural sensibility is the word *power*, specifically the difference of power in the relationship between healthcare providers and patients. In its simplest form, **power** means the ability to do something. Power is neither a bad nor a negative word, and historically in nursing education, sources of power were foundations in nursing curricula. As we explore the relationship between healthcare providers and patients, it is important to acknowledge that a power difference exists. Healthcare providers, regardless of their role, hold the position of power in the relationship. Some readers may immediately ask, "What about patients who threaten to sue healthcare providers, and what about the practice of 'defensive medicine'? Doesn't that mean patients hold the power?"

AUTHOR'S NOTE

Some may be asking, what is defensive medicine? So here is a very brief (and simple) example of **defensive medicine**. Eight-year-old Joshua is rushed to the doctor's office with severe abdominal pain. After a thorough physical assessment, all signs and symptoms point to Joshua eating a bag of his sister's candy. However, knowing an X-ray will reveal nothing unusual, the doctor orders an X-ray that reveals nothing out of the ordinary for an 8-year-old who ate an entire bag of candy. In this example, the X-ray was ordered to demonstrate that all medical assessments were performed. For additional information on this extensive topic, use your favorite search engine and perform a brief review of the literature.

Regardless of the situation, healthcare providers have more power than patients in the provider-patient relationship. Consider, for instance, the following points:

- Healthcare providers possess a specialized language and body of knowledge that in most situations patients do not possess.

- Generally, healthcare providers understand how to navigate within the healthcare system at a greater level of sophistication than individuals seeking healthcare.

- Patients most often enter the healthcare system when they are in physical need of services from healthcare providers. If they are unhappy with the service they receive, they may be unskilled or lack knowledge to secure another provider or seek a second opinion.

- If a healthcare provider does not know how to seek another provider or a second opinion, that provider generally has access to resources about the healthcare system that will allow the provider to obtain another provider or a second opinion.

The preceding four bulleted points highlight the power difference between healthcare providers and patients. If healthcare providers fail to recognize the inherent power difference in the provider-patient relationship, they omit a critical step in providing culturally sensible healthcare. To understand the importance of power difference a little better, consider the following scenario.

Scenario: Mrs. Hill

Mrs. Hill was receiving prenatal care at a large physician practice group whose policy was to have patients meet all the physicians during the last trimester of pregnancy, in case one of them was on call instead of the primary care physician when a woman's labor begins. At her 36-week visit, Mrs. Hill saw Dr. Farley. He had a deep southern drawl and the physical stature of a football player. He was a little scruffy after being up all night with five deliveries. During the visit, Dr. Farley was very concerned with Mrs. Hill's petite frame and a baby that appeared to be large for gestational age. Based on this information, Dr. Farley performed a pelvic exam to assess whether a vaginal delivery was an option. During the pelvic exam, while his hand was in Mrs. Hill's vagina, Dr. Farley loudly stated in his southern drawl, "Well, shoot! It's as big as Texas in here; we don't have to worry."

Additional information: Mrs. Hill is an excellent and very knowledgeable obstetrics and gynecology nurse at a nearby agency. She is assertive and has previously reported a physician for poor communication with patients. Mrs. Hill shared the following with me:

> When that doctor made the big as Texas comment, I was so embarrassed, shocked, humiliated, and I kind

of felt violated. I wondered if he would have made
that comment had my husband been at the visit.
My initial response was to take my foot from the
stirrup and kick him in the face or stomach. I knew
I couldn't reach his groin, but that was really what
I wanted to kick. (short pause) But, I knew better. I
knew he had the control to hurt my vaginal area, the
baby, or worse, be at my delivery and do who knows
what. And you know, as life would have it, he did
end up delivering my baby. I never reported him. (a
long pause) My son is 25; wow, that happened 25
years ago, and I remember it like yesterday. I don't
know if I'll ever forget it. I'll tell you one thing: I
don't let males do pelvic exams on me.

This scenario, like all the scenarios in this guidebook, is true.
This one highlights how powerless a healthcare provider and a
nurse felt when she was in the patient role. Normally, Mrs. Hill
is a woman who speaks up for herself. Yet in the patient role,
she was concerned with retribution to her or her baby if she
shared her concerns with appropriate personnel. If a healthcare
provider can experience this degree of powerlessness, we can
only imagine how "regular" patients might feel in a similar situation. So, we need to consider the importance of recognizing,
appreciating, and valuing the need to respect the power difference in the provider-patient relationship.

I hope this scenario has prompted a wide range of thoughts,
comments, and perhaps emotions. If so, good; it helps us to
think deeply about the practice of healthcare delivery.

Activity: Think About Power Differentials

1. Have you ever heard or seen what's described here?

   - "He's being a bad patient and not doing his suggested walks."

   - "I'm not supposed to let anyone stay after visiting hours, but I'll make an exception."

   - "You have to take your bath in the morning."

   - "You have to take your pain medication now. I'll be busy with another patient for about an hour and won't be able to give you medication until after I've finished."

   - "Don't waste your time trying to educate them about diabetic care; they're noncompliant."

   Describe how these statements, though factual, may represent the nurse's power in the nurse-patient relationship.

   _____

   _____

   _____

   _____

2. The next time you're performing your role as a health-care provider, think about the power you have with pa-tients and families. As you consider the concept of power differential, do you find yourself changing your practice of care during your patient interactions? Use the space here to document your comments.

_____

_____

_____

_____

Summary

Language barriers make communication difficult. A common language for talking about culture is important not only be-cause it limits misunderstandings but also because it may help identify our own prejudices. Language has power, as well. Mak-ing sure that the language we use in healthcare doesn't exert power, cause confusion, or alienate patients is important.

References

Albanese, M. A. (2006). Crafting the reflective lifelong learner: Why, what and how. *Medical Education, 40*, 288–290.

American Nurses Association. (1991). Position statement on cultural diversity in nursing practice. Retrieved from http://www.nursingworld. org/MainMenuCategories/Policy-Advocacy/Positions-and-Resolutions/ ANAPositionStatements/Position-Statements-Alphabetically/prtetcldv14444.html

Cross, T., Bazron, B., Dennis, K., & Isaacs, M. (1989). *Towards A Culturally Competent System of Care*, Volume I. Washington, DC: Georgetown University Child Development Center, CASSP Technical Assistance Center.

Epstein, R. M. (1999). Mindful practice. *JAMA, 282*(9), 833–839.

Learn English Organization. (2013). English horror mistakes. Retrieved from http://www.learnenglish.de/mistakes/HorrorMistakes.html

Leininger, M., & McFarland, M. R. (2002). *Transcultural nursing: Concepts, theories, research & practice*, 3rd ed. New York, NY: McGraw-Hill.

Mamede, S., & Schmidt, H. G. (2004). The structure of reflective practice in medicine. *Medical Education, 38*, 1302–1308.

National Center for Cultural Competence, Georgetown University Center for Child and Human Development, Georgetown University Medical Center. (2004). Bridging the cultural divide in health care settings: The essential role of cultural broker programs. Retrieved from http://gucchd.georgetown.edu/72375.html

National Standards for Culturally and Linguistically Appropriate Services in Health Care Final Report, OMH. (2001). Retrieved from http://minorityhealth.hhs.gov/templates/browse.aspx?lvl=2&lvlID=11

Office of Minority Health U.S. Department of Health & Human Services. (2013). The national standards for culturally and linguistically appropriate services in health and health care: A blueprint for advancing and sustaining CLAS policy and practice. Retrieved from http://minorityhealth.hhs.gov/omh/browse.aspx?lvl=2&lvlid=53

Schön, D. A. (1983). *The reflective practitioner: How professionals think in practice*. New York, NY: Basic Books, Inc.

Tervalon, M., & Murray-Garcia, J. (1998). Cultural humility versus cultural competence: A critical distinction in defining physician training outcomes in multicultural education in the *Journal of Health Care for the Poor and Underserved, 2*, 117–125.

U.S. Department of Health & Human Services. (2010). HealthyPeople.gov, Disparities. Retrieved from http://www.healthypeople.gov/2020/about/disparitiesAbout.aspx

3

LESSENING
THE IMPACT OF
CULTURAL CLASHES

Lions, tigers, and bears are considered some of the most danger-
ous predators on the planet and normally live acrimoniously as
competing predators. Yet at a wild animal reserve in Georgia,
a lion, tiger, and bear live harmoniously together. They've been
together since cubs, when they were rescued from owners who
abused and tortured them. Somehow this unlikely threesome es-
tablished a bridge that allowed them to cross their natural pred-
ator instincts and create a bond that is inseparable, according
to the animal husbandry manager at Noah's Ark (ABC News,
2013). But is crossing cultural differences this easy for humans?

We've passed the first decade of the 21st century, and many of us think nothing about rolling out of our bed in the morning in one state and within a 24-hour period landing in another state or even another part of the world. Advances in communication allow loved ones to communicate anywhere in the world through emails, tweets, Skyping, FaceTime, or an array of other technologies. Even national economies are interconnected. The trade markets of 2012 demonstrated that the economies of the world are interdependent on each other's respective stock markets as national and international recessions loomed as a result of interdependent activities. In this age of global mobility, instant communication, and interconnectedness, diverse cultures are shoved together in multiple sociocultural interactions with and without preparation. If we anticipate that we'll encounter multiple sociocultural interactions, we'll be more prepared to create cultural bridges. But, if we are unprepared, cultural clashes will occur that may create personal scars or erupt into more negative outcomes.

Healthcare: A Fertile Environment for Cultural Clashes

In healthcare environments, diverse cultural interactions occur as healthcare providers are expected to provide culturally appropriate and sensitive healthcare to all individuals in each setting, regardless of their role. But how do healthcare providers provide culturally appropriate and sensitive healthcare when they have personal experiences related to cultural diversity, inclusiveness, race, bigotry, and so on? Even the terminology surrounding culturally appropriate and sensitive healthcare can cause the meekest of healthcare providers to explode with passion for human equality or implode from unresolved emotions. Consequently, healthcare providers may feel overwhelmed, exhausted, and even insulted at the thought that one might assume they would not provide appropriate and sensitive healthcare.

In many healthcare agencies, mandatory cultural diversity and inclusivity training is designed to promote skills and knowledge about specific cultural groups and is often accompanied with a litany of typical cultural responses for various ethnic, racial, and cultural groups. There is nothing wrong with this approach if one is receptive to learning the information. Unfortunately, for many healthcare providers, this creates a déjà vu response instead of empowering them to navigate through potentially complex interactions.

AUTHOR'S NOTE

At this point, I want to emphasize that I am not supporting lessening the importance of political advocacy, human rights issues, social justice, and equality. These issues are critical to a holistic and healthy society. I am proposing cultural sensibility as a practical approach to help healthcare providers prepare for multiple sociocultural interactions.

A DOSE OF REALITY

Imagine someone who has never tasted salt. The taste can be described, the chemical composition diagramed, and a description of all its uses can be documented through recipes. Until salt is experienced by the senses, however, it remains a distant concept. Recently, a 30-something individual viewed a documentary about a traumatic event in world history. The documentary provided a tangible reality about a historical event. The individual's immediate response was, "That really happened! People died! Why didn't they teach us that in school?" The content of the documentary was taught in school, but the audio and cinematography provided a reality to the event for this viewer, and new realities of the circumstances were heartfelt by the observer. Cinematography is not a skill set of this author's. However, the following scenarios are presented in hopes of bringing a new reality to the multiple sociocultural clashes that occur daily and in hopes of reinforcing why cultural sensibility is needed. The scenarios presented are rooted in actual situations. Individual name changes and slight alterations to the scenario were made to maintain anonymity.

Scenarios

Real-life examples can help bring home a point more quickly and clearly than theory. The following scenarios actually occurred. They did not occur in the distant past or during the Civil Rights era of the 1960s. Unfortunately, they reflect modern-day cultural clashes in healthcare. The scenarios are presented in hopes of bringing often-hidden realities to light and highlighting why cultural sensibility is needed. Some scenarios contain derogatory statements and terms. They are included not for shock value, but to help you grasp and perhaps affirm the reality of cultural experiences that occur in healthcare daily. Some scenarios may trigger emotional distress. If this occurs, contact your medical provider, employee assistance program, counselor, or indicated emergency services.

AUTHOR'S NOTE:

Again, I thank the people who shared their experiences and the anger, fear, frustration, and pain that occurred as a result of their experiences with cultural exclusiveness, cultural incompetence, and a lack of cultural humility. I honor and respect their experience by sharing with you their story.

Earletta, Student Nurse

Earletta recalls being assigned to provide nursing care for a 75-year-old gentleman who was alert and oriented to person, place, and time. The primary nurse told her, "Oh, you'll like Mr. Johnson. He is such a sweet man. The entire staff likes him.

We're thrilled with his recovery. All the students have enjoyed working with him. It will be a great learning experience." Earletta was excited for this learning opportunity and thought how gracious Mr. Johnson must be to welcome students as his nurse for the day. Earletta knocked on Mr. Johnson's door and entered the room, offering respectful and appropriate introductions. Mr. Johnson looked at Earletta, leaned forward, and sternly replied, "No foreigner or colored gal is taking care of me!"

> Some may say that Mr. Johnson is old and perhaps suffering from dementia. Others may say that Mr. Johnson is responding from his cultural experiences. There might be other reasons for his response that we don't know. The real issue is: Do faculty openly prepare students for a situation such as this?

Jasmine, RN

Jasmine, a European-American nurse, graduated at the top of her class from one of the most prestigious nursing programs. She's practiced 3 years as a certified nurse in medical-surgical nursing and constantly receives praise from her patients about the care she provides. One day, after making initial rounds, she returned to the nurses' station, sat down, and said the following: "I can take care of any patient, but I can't stand druggie patients. They are no better than poor white trash!" The nurses' station had nurse techs, student nurses, and several RNs present.

> What do Jasmine's colleagues do in this situation?

Dr. Larson

A healthcare system had aggressively recruited Dr. Larson to a rural area with a population of 39,000. The town was located approximately 200 to 300 miles from the two major metropolitan areas closest to it. After careful investigation and counsel with family members and colleagues, Dr. Larson accepted the offer and moved his family to the rural area. A year passed, and they were enjoying their new friends, work life, and community. One day, Dr. Larson was reviewing the physical history of a new patient with gastrointestinal complaints. Dr. Larson asked the patient to describe the color, shape, and general appearance of his bowel movements. The patient paused for a moment, looked at Dr. Larson, and then said, "Well, they look like the color of your dark face."

Much like the scenario with Earletta, was the potential for an interaction of this nature discussed during Dr. Larson's medical school or residency?

Robert, RN

Robert was in school working toward a master's degree as an advanced practice nurse. He and his fellow students were beginning their initial clinical rotation at the university's multiclinic site. As the faculty member led them on a tour of a particular clinic, the staff began to whisper, and then one said, "Do we get the good-looking male nurse in this group?" "Yes, buddy, it will be a joy to come to work for the next 6 weeks!" "Honey, I will be your personal guide, and we'll make sure you pass."

Oh dear, is this sexual harassment?

These scenarios reflect only a few of the many modern-day experiences that describe cultural clashes in healthcare. Even in nursing education, Hassouneh (2006) describes how faculty receive subtle and overt racist feedback on student evaluations, including the use of the term *sand nigger* (a common racist epithet directed toward Arabs and Arab Americans).

Cultural Clashes

The scenarios presented earlier can be interpreted from a variety of perspectives and meanings. Yet each person who shared his or her story was offended, humiliated, and devalued to some degree. Several wondered whether the offender acted deliberately or out of ignorance. Despite their motivation, the offender responded from his or her values and beliefs about the situation; the offenders demonstrated their cultural beliefs. At the core of each scenario, opposing values, beliefs, attitudes, behaviors, and norms (culture) toward the activity, topic, issue, or image the person represented to the other person collided (clashed). That is, cultural clashing occurred. Could the clashing of cultures have been avoided?

Edward T. Hall was the first to present the Cultural Iceberg Model, in 1976 (Constant Foreigner, 2010). Hall compared culture to an iceberg, with only 10% to 20% of cultural attributes visible above the water's surface and the remainder hidden below, like an iceberg (see Figure 3.1). The two levels of his cultural iceberg were conscious behaviors (visible) and unconscious (hidden). The conscious behaviors included cultural behaviors that reflected traditions, customs, and those areas easily learned and generally observable by others through the observer's five senses. The hidden, below the iceberg, cultural behaviors that comprised 80% to 90% of one's culture were not only difficult to change, but difficult to observe. Behaviors below the iceberg reflect our core values, assumptions, attitudes, and beliefs. Hall further proposed that to know the 80% to 90% of another's hidden culture, one must don the role of a learner and spend time in the other culture. Hall's idea is theoretically simple and logical, but labor-intensive in the time-restrained, high-volume healthcare interactions we face today.

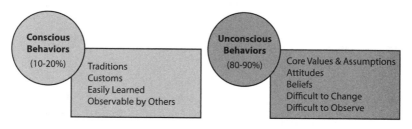

Figure 3.1   Components of Hall's Cultural Iceberg Model

Let's exam the scenario about Mrs. Hill, from Chapter 2, "Common Ground: Terms and Definitions," using the perspective of Hall's Cultural Iceberg Model. Her experience is repeated here for your review.

Mrs. Hill was receiving prenatal care at a large physician practice group whose policy was to have patients meet all the physicians during the last trimester of pregnancy, in case one of them was on call instead of the primary care physician when a woman's labor begins. At her 36-week visit, Mrs. Hill saw Dr. Farley. He had a deep southern drawl and the physical stature of a football player. He was a little scruffy after being up all night with five deliveries. During the visit, Dr. Farley was very concerned with Mrs. Hill's petite frame and a baby that appeared to be large for gestational age. Based on this information, Dr. Farley performed a pelvic exam to assess whether a vaginal delivery was an option. During the pelvic exam, while his hand was in Mrs. Hill's vagina, Dr. Farley loudly stated in his southern drawl, "Well, shoot! It's as big as Texas in here; we don't have to worry."

Using the following table, I've grouped potential conscious and unconscious behavior for Mrs. Hill and Dr. Farley into conscious and unconscious behaviors using Hall's Cultural Iceberg Model.

Conscious Behaviors		Unconscious Behaviors	
Traditions, Customs, Easily Learned, Observable by Others		**Core Values and Assumptions, Attitudes, Beliefs, Difficult to Change, Difficult to Observe**	
Mrs. Hill	*Dr. Farley*	*Mrs. Hill*	*Dr. Farley*
Physician will appear well groomed and professional.	Reassure patient regarding delivery.	Suspicious of male physicians resulting from previous negative experiences.	Third pregnancy.
Physician will introduce himself to me.	Third pregnancy; there should be few questions.	Prefers female doctors.	Obstetrical visit should be very quick.
Physician will review and agree with my birth plan.		Protocol and etiquette are highly valued.	Staying on schedule is important.
		A slow southern drawl may mean one is less competent and lacks assurance in one's decisions.	Running 30 minutes behind from the last delivery.
			Very concerned with Mrs. Hill's petite frame and a large-for-gestational-age fetus.
			She may be a candidate for a C-section.
			As big as Texas is a phrase that Dr. Farley uses to describe many things.

In reviewing the conscious behavioral list, you can see that Mrs. Hill has very specific expectations for the obstetrical visit that differed from Dr. Farley's anticipated quick visit. With information from the conscious level, we might anticipate that Mrs. Hill or Dr. Farley may be frustrated with the outcome of the visit. However, information from the unconscious level identifies core assumptions by both individuals who are heading for a cultural clash that potentially may result in a less-than-optimal obstetrical visit. In the real-life version of this scenario, Mrs. Hill felt insulted and embarrassed that her pelvis (in her mind, vagina) would be announced as the size of Texas. Dr. Farley's comment further reinforced Mrs. Hall's distrust of male physicians. The well-meaning, lighthearted comment by Dr. Farley was intended to provide reassurance to Mrs. Hill. Unfortunately, she had no idea this communication pattern by Dr. Farley was his way to convey the assessment from the pelvic exam that her pelvic measures should be more than adequate for a vaginal delivery. Regretfully, the end result from this encounter was a cultural clash experience and an unsatisfactory obstetrical visit for Mrs. Hill. Even 20 years later, Mrs. Hill can describe the incident in exact detail. Dr. Farley never even knew he offended Mrs. Hill. She felt powerless as the patient and only complained to her friends.

Thus we define **cultural clashing** as individuals or groups that have opposing cultures (values, beliefs, attitudes, behaviors, norms, and so on) toward a same issue, topic, or activity.

Activity: Analyze the Mrs. Hill and Dr. Farley Cultural Clash

In the table, try to identify other issues that might have led to a cultural clash between Mrs. Hill and Dr. Farley.

Conscious Behaviors		Unconscious Behaviors	
Traditions, Customs, Easily Learned, Observable by Others		Core Values and Assumptions, Attitudes, Beliefs, Difficult to Change, Difficult to Observe	
Mrs. Hill	Dr. Farley	Mrs. Hill	Dr. Farley

Activity: Reflection or What If

Healthcare providers prepare for cardiac arrest through preparation and thinking through potential scenarios. A major component of cultural sensibility is reflection.

1. Reread the scenarios. As you do, imagine yourself being on the receiving end of the insults.

2. Jot down your responses in the spaces provided.

_____

_____

_____

_____

3. Reflect on your answers after recording them. It's important to imagine what you might say or feel in these situations because it helps you prepare for similar or actual situations. Remember that preparation helps minimize the chances of cultural clashing.

Earletta, Student Nurse

Earletta recalls being assigned to provide nursing care for a 75-year-old gentleman who was alert and oriented to person, place, and time. The primary nurse told her, "Oh, you'll like Mr. Johnson. He is such a sweet man. The entire staff likes him. We're thrilled with his recovery. All the students have enjoyed working with him. It will be a great learning experience." Earletta was excited for this learning opportunity and thought how gracious Mr. Johnson must be to welcome students as his nurse for the day. Earletta knocked on Mr. Johnson's door and entered the room, offering respectful and appropriate introductions. Mr. Johnson looked at Earletta, leaned forward, and sternly replied, "No foreigner or colored gal is taking care of me!"

- What would you want to say? What would you actually say?

  _____

  _____

  _____

  _____

- How would you respond?

  _____

  _____

  _____

  _____

- Would you be able to retain focus on the task at hand?

_____

_____

_____

_____

Jasmine, RN

Jasmine, a European-American nurse, graduated at the top of her class from one of the most prestigious nursing programs. She's practiced 3 years as a certified nurse in medical-surgical nursing and constantly receives praise from her patients about the care she provides. One day, after making initial rounds, she returned to the nurses' station, sat down, and said the following: "I can take care of any patient, but I can't stand druggie patients. They are no better than poor white trash!" The nurses' station had nurse techs, student nurses, and several RNs present.

- What would you want to say? What would you actually say?

_____

_____

_____

_____

- How would you respond?

_____

_____

_____

_____

• Would you be able to retain focus on the task at hand?

_____

_____

_____

_____

Dr. Larson

A healthcare system had aggressively recruited Dr. Larson to a rural area with a population of 39,000. The town was located approximately 200 to 300 miles from the two major metropolitan areas closest to it. After careful investigation and counsel with family members and colleagues, Dr. Larson accepted the offer and moved his family to the rural area. A year passed, and they were enjoying their new friends, work life, and community. One day, Dr. Larson was reviewing the physical history of a new patient with gastrointestinal complaints. Dr. Larson asked the patient to describe the color, shape, and general appearance of his bowel movements. The patient paused for a moment, looked at Dr. Larson, and then said, "Well, they look like the color of your dark face."

• What would you want to say? What would you actually say?

_____

_____

_____

_____

- How would you respond?

_____

_____

_____

_____

- Would you be able to retain focus on the task at hand?

_____

_____

_____

_____

Robert, RN

Robert was in school working toward a master's degree as an advanced practice nurse. He and his fellow students were beginning their initial clinical rotation at the university's multiclinic site. As the faculty member led them on a tour of a particular clinic, the staff began to whisper, and then one said, "Do we get the good-looking male nurse in this group?" "Yes, buddy, it will be a joy to come to work for the next 6 weeks!" "Honey, I will be your personal guide, and we'll make sure you pass."

- What would you want to say? What would you actually say?

_____

_____

_____

_____

- How would you respond?

  _____

  _____

  _____

  _____

- Would you be able to retain focus on the task at hand?

  _____

  _____

  _____

  _____

Mrs. Hill

Mrs. Hill was receiving prenatal care at a large physician practice group whose policy was to have patients meet all the physicians during the last trimester of pregnancy, in case one of them was on call instead of the primary care physician when a woman's labor begins. At her 36-week visit, Mrs. Hill saw Dr. Farley. He had a deep southern drawl and the physical stature of a football player. He was a little scruffy after being up all night with five deliveries. During the visit, Dr. Farley was very concerned with Mrs. Hill's petite frame and a baby that appeared to be large for gestational age. Based on this information, Dr. Farley performed a pelvic exam to assess whether a vaginal delivery was an option. During the pelvic exam, while his hand was in Mrs. Hill's vagina, Dr. Farley loudly stated in his southern drawl, "Well, shoot! It's as big as Texas in here; we don't have to worry."

- What would you want to say? What would you actually say?

  _____

  _____

  _____

  _____

- How would you respond?

  _____

  _____

  _____

  _____

- Would you be able to retain focus on the task at hand?

  _____

  _____

  _____

  _____

Activity: Examine Someone's Cultural Iceberg

By this point in the chapter, you should now have a basic understanding of cultural clashing. Recall a recent cultural clash between two individuals. See whether you can identify the conscious and unconscious cultural behaviors without stereotyping either person. (Hint: Avoiding the temptation to stereotype is very challenging.)

Conscious Behaviors		Unconscious Behaviors	
Traditions, Customs, Easily Learned, Observable by Others		Core Values and Assumptions, Attitudes, Beliefs, Difficult to Change, Difficult to Observe	
Person 1	Person 2	Person 1	Person 2

Avoiding Cultural Clashes

The scenarios previously presented are encounters heading toward cultural clashes. How could the clashing of cultures have been prevented? Unfortunately, it is not as easy as step one, step two, and so on. No cookie-cutter response will fit every situation and produce a positive outcome. Simply put, the avoidance of cultural clashes cannot be a one-size-fits-all formula. Each of us is in a different place in our respective growth and development regarding recognizing, addressing, and responding to cultural issues in healthcare. The simplest steps we can take as healthcare providers is to respond sensibly by applying critical thinking skills and becoming a reflective-in-action healthcare provider.

This guidebook identifies ways to navigate through professional expectations and personal experiences toward providing culturally appropriate and sensitive healthcare. It is designed for those seeking to enhance their behavior in this area. It is not a textbook. It is not loaded with theories, and it is not a psychotherapy book. It is a guidebook for a personal journey toward providing **culturally sensible healthcare**, with an emphasis on *sensible*. The guidebook draws on more than 30 years of nursing experience and lifelong experience as a female from a historically underrepresented population. The discussions presented on cultural sensibility have not been tested as a theoretical framework or presented with measurable outcomes from the author's research. And please be aware that *cultural sensibility* is not "my" term. Dogra (2003) coined the term.

The concept of cultural sensibility is offered as a practical healthcare behavioral approach for patient-consumer interactions. Cultural sensibility is not a journey by which one will arrive and become culturally sensible. It is a behavior, an attitude that a healthcare provider elects to embrace during patient interactions. If you are seeking books on specific cultural groups, there are many great references that exist and can be identified by using any of the current search engines. However, it is this author's belief that you can never know every cultural group and the variety of subcultures within any identified group. Therefore, a culturally sensible approach to providing culturally appropriate and sensitive healthcare may be more effective. So, with this review, the journey toward cultural sensibility continues.

AUTHOR'S NOTE

The term *patient* can convey a dependent role without power, and at times during the healthcare experience, as in emergencies, this may be true. The term *consumer* can convey an individual with greater power to choose services and have a voice. The author's personal preference is the word consumer. However, the distinction between patient and consumer is not the focus for this guidebook. Because the more common term in healthcare delivery is patient, that's what you'll find throughout this guidebook.

Culturally Appropriate and Sensitive Healthcare

In the United States, culturally appropriate healthcare is predominately rooted in research findings under the broad topic of healthcare disparities. The most notable findings on healthcare disparities in the United States were published by the Institute of Medicine (2002) in the book *Unequal Treatment: Confronting Racial and Ethnic Disparities in Healthcare*. The primary premise of the report was "that even at equivalent levels of access to care, racial and ethnic minorities experience a lower quality of health services and are less likely to receive even routine medical procedures" (pp. 29–30). The book also documents the unequal healthcare treatment provided to various ethnic and racial groups. This groundbreaking report also presented recommendations to address healthcare disparities. Other reports had been presented earlier, but from this author's perspective, *Unequal Treatment* launched a national examination of how the healthcare system and providers address healthcare disparities and unequal treatment in the delivery of healthcare services. As a result, recommendations and standards supporting equal healthcare treatment regardless of ethnicity, gender, race, age, primary language, or sexual orientation/gender identity are becoming the norm throughout the healthcare environment.

The U.S. Department of Health & Human Services Office of Minority Health (http://minorityhealth.hhs.gov/), The Joint Commission (http://www.jointcommission.org/), the American Association of Colleges of Nursing (http://www.aacn.nche.edu/), and the Liaison Committee on Medical Education (http://www.lcme.org/), in addition to various state and local agencies, address the need for healthcare providers to be culturally appropriate and sensitive in providing healthcare. Organizations that are homogeneous in gender, ethnicity, race, or culture are accountable to demonstrate how they meet current recommendations and standards for their agencies in providing culturally appropriate and sensitive healthcare. The following activities will reinforce the concepts we've discussed so far in this chapter.

Activity: Tug-A-Win-A University

Part A: Imagine that you are in a foreign country on a very crowded street. You're by yourself, and you do not speak the language. You are even dressed differently from the locals from head to toe. The customs and practices are different from what you are used to, and to make things worse, you are very hungry but cannot find a restaurant. You've tried to start conversations, verbally and nonverbally, but so far without success.

1. List the emotions you would experience in the situation just described.

   _____

   _____

2. Now review the list of emotions you've selected.

   _____

   _____

3. Describe how reviewing the preceding list makes you feel.

_____

_____

Part B: You are wearing your favorite university T-shirt from Tug-A-Win-A University. During your tenure at Tug-A-Win-A, you were busy working full time, caring for members in your support system, and had little time for extracurricular activities or school spirit. You will never be voted alum of the year, but the T-shirt is very comfortable to wear and is easy to pack.

Suddenly in the distance (like in any story), coming toward you... Yes, it is getting clearer. You see someone wearing a T-shirt from Tug-A-Win-A University.

1. Now write a new list of emotions you experience when seeing a total stranger wearing a T-shirt like yours from Tug-A-Win-A University.

_____

_____

2. Review the list of emotions you previously identified.

_____

_____

3. Do you see a difference in the list?

_____

_____

Many of us in Part A would initially feel isolated, overwhelmed, or even scared. However, the sight of another person who evokes a point of familiarity, as described in Part B, generally prompts us to gravitate toward that person, even if we do not know him or her. Upon meeting, you might find that the other T-shirt wearer gets on your nerves (for whatever reasons), but you might decide to overlook his or her annoying characteristics and even spend time traveling together, no matter how briefly. (You might travel with the person at least to the nearest restaurant, if he or she knows where it is.)

BELONGING, FEELING COMFORTABLE TO BE ME

Beverly Daniel Tatum (1997) wrote a book with a fascinating title, *"Why Are All the Black Kids Sitting Together in the Cafeteria?"* This book is mentioned here not as any type of book review, but instead to just focus on the title. In years past, unfortunately, I heard faculty at all academic levels express almost verbatim this title when students from similar cultural groups were present in small numbers (the minority) in a homogeneous majority setting and the minority group sat together in class or breakrooms. In reality, any small group that is not part of the homogeneous majority group, seeking similarity (age, gender, class, race, geographic representation, and so on), will cluster together in most every setting. Why? The simplest answer is this: The group represented in small numbers is searching for a point of commonality that brings comfort, a sense of sameness or belonging that most of us seek in various forms at different points in our life. However, that simple act of seeking sameness by a small group may be viewed by the homogeneous majority as an act of defiance, cliquish, or an array of other descriptors.

Part C

Review the complete scenario, Part A and Part B, along with your responses to the questions.

- Can you recall a situation that reflects the situation described? If yes, which group did you belong to, the minority or majority group?

  _____

  _____

- Did you secretly want to belong to the other group?

  _____

  _____

Let's return to the two individuals with Tug-A-Win-A University T-shirts.

- First, remove the fictitious T-shirts and transport the two individuals from that country into your healthcare practice setting.

- Second, envision the two individuals as a part of the minority population of your healthcare practice setting.

  Decide whether they are individuals who represent a minority patient population *or* a minority population of healthcare providers, workers, or staff in your healthcare practice setting. One minority could be the population that has English as a second language.

- Third, write how you honestly view these two individuals.

  Do you view them differently?

  Dig below the surface politically correct response and ask yourself the hard question: "Do I view them differently?"

  Describe why you do or you don't view them differently.

  It doesn't matter whether or not you view them differently. What is important is to examine the situation, reflect on how you view them, and determine why you view them the way that you do.

Here's a different example from my past. I used to be fearful of climbing "open" stairs. When I asked myself why, I remembered my mother saying, "Be careful going up these steps. They are open, and I don't want you to fall through." Well, for years, I was afraid that I would fall through any staircase that did not have a riser. Finally, I realized I was too big to fall through. (Historically, stairs without risers were most common on fire stairs outside of buildings, as pictured in Figure 3.2.) I hope this example helps you recall why you responded as you did to Parts A through C of this activity.

Figure 3.2   Fire Escape Stairs Without Risers

If you fully embrace the reflection activity, you should begin to remember verbal and nonverbal messages that influence the perceptions and beliefs you have toward this situation. Some may call this "messages from your past." The exercise was not about right or wrong. In very simple steps, this section presented fundamental aspects of belonging, culture, diversity, and perceptions. The goal was to acknowledge your culturally unique perspectives about the situation described.

In 1998, Giger and Davidhizar developed the Transcultural Assessment Model to assist student nurses in recognizing the culturally unique attributes of individuals. The developers began with the concept of the culturally unique individual that described all humans as culturally unique by their cultural and racial identification, place of birth, and the events occurring in the country when they were born and raised. They further describe that individuals are influenced by six cultural phenomena:

- Biological variations
- Environmental control
- Time
- Social orientation
- Space
- Communication

In today's healthcare environment, time restrictions may not afford the luxury of completing a Transcultural Assessment Model as described by Giger and Davidhizar. Acknowledging the culturally unique individuality of each of us, even from the same family, tribe, ethnic, or geographic group, is an initial step toward cultural sensibility.

Summary

Based on Hall's Cultural Iceberg Model, we continually risk cultural clashes because we generally respond to the 10% to 20% of cultural behaviors we see. In reality, though, an individual may be operating from the 80% to 90% of cultural behaviors that are unseen. Recognizing this discrepancy can help us to remember that we are seeing just a small glimpse of the real person and we may only be revealing a small glimpse of the real us to the other person. Cultural clashes may or may not be avoidable, but failure to effectively resolve them can leave lifelong impressions. At the core of each of us, we need to belong and be recognized. Healthcare encounters are focused interactions, but these same issues are ever-present.

References

ABC News. (2013). Three fierce predators living together. Retrieved from http://abcnews.go.com/WNT/video/lions-tigers-bears-living-18928105

Constant Foreigner (2010). Edward T. Hall's cultural iceberg model. Retrieved from http://constantforeigner.com/research/edward-t-halls-cultural-iceberg/

Dogra, N. (2003). Cultural expertise or cultural sensibility? A comparison of two ideal type models to teach cultural diversity to medical students. *International Journal of Medicine, 5*(4), 223–231.

Giger, J. N., & Davidhizar, R. E. (1999). *Transcultural nursing: Assessment & intervention.* St. Louis, MO: Mosby.

Hassouneh, D. (2006). Anti-racist pedagogy: Challenges faced by faculty of color in predominantly white schools of nursing. *Journal of Nursing Education, 45*(7), 255–262.

Smedley, B. D., Stith, A. Y., & Nelson, A. R. (Eds.) (2003). *Unequal treatment: Confronting racial and ethnic disparities in health care.* Washington, DC: The National Academies Press.

4

HEALTHCARE DISPARITIES: THEY AFFECT US ALL

In September 2013, I used OvidSP to search for the topic *healthcare disparities*. I was looking for new articles on the subject. The search returned 7,672 results. Eagerly, I reviewed the results and discovered that 7 of the first 10 articles covered healthcare disparities from a broader perspective than just in the United States. The findings from this search are an excellent reminder that healthcare disparities are nondiscriminatory; they affect us all.

Globally, social determinants often systemically limit, hinder, or even block access to healthcare. The findings from this search on the topic of healthcare disparities, listed in the following table, identified populations from Australia, Canada, Chile, China, and Senegal that are impacted by healthcare disparities. The global phenomenon of inadequate healthcare access, delivery, and outcomes may differ from country to country, but the global goal to reduce such disparities is this: *equity in care.*

Authors	Year	Title	Journal
Jovic, L., Lecordier, D., Mottaz, A. M., & Deme, D. V.	2013	Live from Melbourne, the 25th Four-Year Meeting of the International Council of Nurses: Equity and Access to Health Care [French]	*Recherche en Soins Infirmiers (Research in Nursing), (113)*5, Editorial
Thackrah, R. D., & Thompson, S. C.	2013	Refining the Concept of Cultural Competence: Building on Decades of Progress [Discusses disparities in health outcomes among indigenous Australians]	*Medical Journal of Australia, 199*(1), 35–38
Espinoza, I., Thomson, W. M., Gamonal, J., & Arteaga, O.	2013	Disparities in Aspects of Oral-Health-Related Quality of Life Among Chilean Adults	*Community Dentistry & Oral Epidemiology, 41*(3), 242–250
Ramraj C., & Quinonez, C. R.	2013	Self-Reported Cost-Prohibitive Dental Care Needs Among Canadians	*International Journal of Dental Hygiene, 11*(2), 115–120

Authors	Year	Title	Journal
King, N. B., & Fraser, V.	2013	Untreated Pain, Narcotics Regulation, and Global Health Ideologies	*PLoS Medicine / Public Library of Science, 10*(4):e1001411
Zhang, X., Xiong, Y., Ye, J., Deng, Z., & Zhang, X.	2013	Analysis of Government Investment in Primary Healthcare Institutions to Promote Equity During the Three-Year Health Reform Program in China	*BMC Health Services Research, 13,* 114
Faye, A., Diouf, M., Niang, K., Leye, M. M., Ndiaye, S., Ayad, M., & Tal-Dia, A.	2013	Social Inequality and Antenatal Care: Impact of Economic Welfare on Pregnancy Monitoring in Senegal	*Revue d'Epidemiologie et de Sante Publique* (Epidemiology and Public Health Journal) *61*(2), 180–185

Social Determinants of Health

The term *health disparities* was defined in Chapter 2, "Common Ground: Terms and Definitions," as follows:

A particular type of health difference that is closely linked with social, economic, and/or environmental disadvantage. Health disparities adversely affect groups of people who have systematically experienced greater obstacles to health based on their racial or ethnic group; religion; socioeconomic status; gender; age; mental health; cognitive, sensory, or physical disability; sexual orientation or gender identity;

geographic location; or other characteristics historically linked to discrimination or exclusion
(HealthyPeople.gov, 2013).

Making direct-care providers understand the implications of
healthcare disparities can prove challenging. At the root of the
disparities/inequality in healthcare are five areas that comprise
social determinants of health:

- **Economic stability** refers to the degree to which poverty is present or absent, employment stability, access to
  employment, and recognitions of secure and unsecure
  housing.

- **Education** refers to graduation rates from high school,
  the minimal level of education; policies within school
  systems that support the promotion of health and wellness; school environments where safety is promoted as
  a means to create an optimal learning environment; and
  the percentages of individuals in the community who
  seek, enroll, and obtain education beyond high school.

- **Social and community context** refers to family struc-
  tures, social cohesion, sensitivity to discrimination and
  equity, participation in civic activities, and incarceration
  and institutionalization rates.

- **Health and healthcare** refers to access to health services,
  the development of preventive healthcare initiatives,
  access to primary care for community-based health promotion and wellness programs, and health technology
  access and literacy.

- **Neighborhood and built environment** refers to the quality of housing, levels of violence and crime, environmental conditions, and access to healthful foods.

- Note that these five areas influence healthcare from birth (and often even before conception) to death and that the social determinants of health are interconnected, as shown in Figure 4.1 (an adapted version of how the U.S. Department of Health & Human Services illustrates the interconnectedness of these factors).

Figure 4.1 Social Determinants of Health

The Economic Determinant

The social determinants described in the preceding section apply to all socioeconomic groups, but it is inequality in these areas that leads to disparities in healthcare. To explore social determinants in greater detail, let's examine the economic determinant and the impact of earning only the federal minimum wage. Since 2009, the U.S. federal minimum wage has been $7.25 per hour, which creates an annual income of approximately $15,080, before taxes, based on full-time employment. Some states have a higher minimum wage. For example, in Illinois, the minimum wage is $8.25 ($17,160 annually). In Washington, it is $9.32 ($19,385 annually) (U.S. Department of Labor, 2013; Doyle, 2013).

You might be surprised (unless you are currently earning minimum wage or have done so recently) to learn that minimum wage earners exist in most work sectors classified by the Bureau of Labor Statistics for 2012. The work sectors listed in the following table derive from the *Labor Force Statistics from the Current Population Survey, Characteristics of Minimum Wage Workers 2012.*

Occupation Category	Breakdown
Management, Professional, and Related	Management, business, and financial operations occupations
Service	Healthcare support occupations
	Protective service occupations
	Food preparation and serving-related occupations
	Building and grounds cleaning and maintenance occupations
	Personal care and service occupations
Sales and Office	Sales related
	Office administrative support
Natural Resources, Construction, and Maintenance	Farming, fishing, and forestry
	Construction and extraction
	Installation maintenance and repair
Production Transportation and Material Moving	Production
	Transportation material moving

Occupation Category	Breakdown
Private Sector	Agriculture and related industries
	Mining
	Construction
	Manufacturing durable and nondurable goods
	Wholesale and retail trade
	Transportation and utilities
	Information
	Financial activities
	Professional business services
	Education services
	Health services
	Leisure and hospitality

This table does not list specific jobs with the various sectors that pay minimum wage. Instead, it identifies the sectors themselves where the U.S. Department of Labor has indicated the presence of minimum wage workers. Fast-food workers, sales clerks, certified nursing aids, childcare workers, and administrative assistants are often paid minimum wage (or less, perhaps because not all their hours are counted, for instance).

AUTHOR'S NOTE

Salaries are often influenced, in most sectors, by an applicant's previous experience, education, negotiation skills, and local salary trends.

Activity: Budget as a Low-Wage Earner

Let's consider the budget for a healthcare assistant who earns $8.25 per hour ($17,160 annually). We'll use standard percentages for establishing a household budget from Intuit Quicken (2013) guides. Jessica, our hypothetical healthcare assistant, has a monthly gross (before taxes) income of $1,430. If we subtract approximately 28% ($400) for federal, state, and local taxes; Medicare; Social Security; and workplace benefits, Jessica is left with $1,030 (net/take-home pay).

Household Budget Percentage Allowance	Monthly Net Pay: $1,030
30% Housing	$309.00
10% Utilities and other housing expenditures (including renters insurance)	103.00
15% Food (at home and away)	154.50
10% Transportation (including car loan)	103.00
10% Debt repayment (student loans and credit cards)	103.00
10% Saving	103.00
5% Clothing	51.50
5% Entertainment	51.50
5% Car insurance and miscellaneous personal expenses	51.50

Examine carefully the monthly allocations for each budget item.

1. Consider whether you could live on this monthly budget if earning $8.25 per hour.

   If this is your approximate income, how close are you to the recommended budget?

2. Using the area where you reside, do a quick Internet search for monthly housing at $309.

3. Evaluate the search results based on the safety of the neighborhoods identified.

   Include the other social determinant factors as evaluation criteria. For instance, consider the following:

   - Education opportunities and graduation rates

   - Family and social stabilities

   - Receptiveness to cultural and ethnic diversity

   - Grocery stores with reasonable cost for fresh fruits and vegetables

   What quality of healthcare services is available in the neighborhoods you determined were affordable?

   Are there safe and well-lit walking areas?

   Is there access to complimentary health services and over-the-counter remedies?

4. Now consider that Jessica is the sole support for her family. Using the 2013 poverty guidelines listed here, determine how many household members Jessica can support before meeting poverty guidelines.

Persons in Family/Household	Poverty Guideline
For families/households with more than 8 persons, add $4,160 for each additional person.	
1	$11,770
2	$15,930
3	$20,090
4	$24,250
5	$28,410
6	$32,570
7	$36,730
8	$40,890

(U.S. Department of Health & Human Services. Office of the Assistant Secretary for Planning and Evaluation, 2015)

Healthcare Provider Power

Now that we've reviewed how one of the social determinants can impact individuals, let's discuss our role as healthcare providers, specifically with a focus on healthcare disparities. Social determinants are inextricably linked to healthcare disparities. Recognizing that, our goal as healthcare providers must be to eliminate (or at least diminish as much as possible) healthcare disparities by providing quality care that is efficient, effective, safe, timely, patient-centered, and equitable. These six qualities, which are described in the following list, are considered by experts as key principles of quality healthcare, with equity as perhaps the most critical and overlooked area by healthcare agencies and leaders:

- **Efficient:** Decrease/avoid wasting supplies, ideas, energy, and resources.

- **Effective:** Services are rooted in evidence-based practice and are not over- or underused.

- **Safe:** Avoid injuries from interventions that are designed to promote wellness and healing.

- **Timely:** Provide care that decreases waits and harmful delays for both patients and providers.

- **Patient-centered:** Recognize, respect, and respond to the individuality of patient needs in the healthcare plan.

- **Equitable:** "Providing care that does not vary in quality because of personal characteristics such as ethnicity, gender, geographic location and socioeconomic status" (The Disparities Solutions Center, Massachusetts General Hospital, 2008, p. 14).

As healthcare providers, we generally want to believe that we treat all patients the same. But, as previously discussed, we each have preferences, biases, and stereotypes that influence our interactions with patients and colleagues (and people in general). In Chapter 3, "Lessening the Impact of Cultural Clashes," you read about Jasmine, RN. Her story is repeated here for this discussion:

> Jasmine, a European-American nurse, graduated at the top of her class from one of the most prestigious nursing programs. She's practiced 3 years as a certified nurse in medical-surgical nursing and constantly receives praise from her patients about the care she provides. One day, after making initial rounds, she returned to the nurses' station, sat down, and said the following: "I can take care of any patient, but I can't stand druggie patients. They are no better than poor white trash!"

Initially, we might say that Jasmine was just having a bad day. Upon further reflection, though, we might determine that Jasmine really does have biases against drug addicts. We also recognize that she has stereotyped all drug addicts as *poor white trash*, not exactly an endearing term.

AUTHOR'S NOTE

The phrase *poor white trash* can be traced to the writings of Ulysses S. Grant (in his memoirs in 1885): "The great bulk of the legal voters of the South were men who owned no slaves; their homes were generally in the hills and poor country; their facilities for educating their children, even up to the point of reading and writing, were very limited; their interest in the contest was very meager—what there was, if they had been capable of seeing it, was with the North; they too needed emancipation. Under the old régime they were looked down upon by those who controlled all the affairs in the interest of slave-owners, as poor white trash who were allowed the ballot so long as they cast it according to direction" (StackExchange, 2013). The Online Slang Dictionary (n.d.) updates and expands the meaning, thusly: "Poor, uneducated Caucasians. They live in filth (e.g. rusting cars and old kitchen appliances fill the front yard), they are poorly educated, they don't care about their appearance (e.g. they are poorly groomed and overweight, wear dirty and tattered clothes), etc. Though 'white trash' can live anywhere, they are indigenous to the Midwestern and southern United States."

In this scenario, Jasmine is not providing equitable healthcare. The quality of her nursing care varies based on the personal characteristics of individuals who are addicted to drugs. By not providing equitable healthcare to those with drug addictions:

- Jasmine is ignoring the social determinants of health that result in gaps for this population.

- Her inability to care for drug-addicted persons will more than likely hinder those patients from receiving critical healthcare information.

- Jasmine's inability to recognize the social determinants of health and the need to care for drug-addicted patients will decrease effectiveness, safety, timeliness, patient-centered care, and efficiency in the delivery of her patients' healthcare.

Jasmine needs a mentor, a liaison, a bridge builder—someone who provides her with a safe environment (safe-zone coach) to explore her biases and stereotypes as a first step toward activating her potential for cultural sensibility. Without a mentor, liaison, or bridge builder, Jasmine will likely continue to ignore social determinants and thus perpetuate healthcare disparities for drug-addicted persons she encounters.

Jasmine is one nurse, but each of us has a Jasmine bias and stereotype that is powerful within us. The most critical action we can take to address this issue is exactly what we're doing right now: We are learning to improve the quality of the healthcare we provide through culturally sensible interactions.

Summary

This chapter examined the concept of disparities in healthcare. As you learned, such disparities can affect us all, and social determinants of health greatly influence both our access to healthcare and the quality of that care (if received at all). Failure to recognize these social determinants of health may result in the perpetuation of stereotypes/biases against already marginalized populations (drug addicts were the example in this chapter). So, as healthcare providers, we should remain vigilant and check our own stereotypes/biases and seek to provide quality care in the most equitable way possible.

References

The Disparities Solutions Center, Massachusetts General Hospital (2008). Improving quality & achieving equity: A guide for hospital leaders. Retrieved from http://www2.massgeneral.org/disparitiessolutions/guide.html

Doyle, A. (2013). List of minimum wage rates for 2014. About.com Job Searching. Retrieved from http://jobsearch.about.com/od/minimumwage/a/minimum-wage-rates-2014.htm

Intuit Quicken (2013). Home budget: Cost-of-living reality check. Article ID: INF 16169. Retrieved from http://quicken.intuit.com/support/help/budgeting-basics/home-budget--cost-of-living-reality-check/INF16169.html;jsessionid=FrRt9nj+zD7c3PIYc7N8Vw**.pprdestas40a-5

Online Slang Dictionary (n.d.). White trash. Retrieved from http://onlineslangdictionary.com/meaning-definition-of/white-trash

StackExchange (2013). English language & usage. Retrieved from http://english.stackexchange.com/questions/41778/what-is-the-early-recorded-use-of-white-trash-and-has-its-meaning-changed-over

U.S. Department of Health & Human Services. Office of the Assistant Secretary for Planning and Evaluation. (2013). Poverty guidelines. Retrieved from http://aspe.hhs.gov/poverty/13poverty.cfm

U.S. Department of Health & Human Services. The secretary's advisory committee on national health promotion and disease prevention objectives for 2020. Phase I report: Recommendations for the framework and format of healthy people 2020. Section IV. Advisory committee findings and recommendations. Retrieved from http://www.healthypeople.gov/2020/about/disparitiesAbout.aspx

U.S. Department of Health & Human Services. Social determinants of health. (n.d.) Retrieved from http://www.healthypeople.gov/2020/topics-objectives/topic/social-determinants-health

U.S. Department of Labor, Bureau of Labor Statistics (2012). Labor force statistics from the current population survey. Characteristics of characteristics of minimum wage workers: 2012. Retrieved from http://www.bls.gov/cps/minwage2012.htm

U.S. Department of Labor, Wage and Hour Division. (n.d.) Minimum wage. Retrieved from http://www.dol.gov/whd/minimumwage.htm

5

BRACKETING, CRITICAL THINKING, AND REFLECTION-IN-ACTION

As you've learned throughout this guidebook, cultural sensibility derives from deliberate, proactive behavior. We have to work to educate ourselves (and others) to reflect. When we become aware of our preconceived ideas and biases but strive to separate our personal beliefs from the provider-patient interaction, we can start providing culturally appropriate healthcare. Because healthcare workers know they will interact with different cultures, preparation is important.

Biases, Prejudices, and Stereotypes

As healthcare providers, we determine the essence of the healthcare we deliver. We affect the consumer experience of our care, and our biases, prejudices, and stereotypes (BPS) also impact discrepancies and disparities in healthcare outcomes.

The seminal and in-depth work by Smedley, Stith, and Nelson (2002) in *Unequal Treatment: Confronting Racial and Ethnic Disparities in Healthcare* states that "healthcare providers' diagnostic and treatment decisions, as well as their feelings about patients are influenced by patients' race or ethnicity" (p. 11). Their work compiled studies from the late 1990s and early 2000s that highlight differences in care based on gender, race, and ethnicity (differences that not only impacted patient outcomes but also led to increased costs in healthcare). Those authors further argued that the sources of healthcare disparities are multilayered, as presented in an integrated model of healthcare disparities. That model highlights three major sources that influence healthcare disparities:

- Unique cultural attributes of the patient

- Provider clarity and interpretation of healthcare data available

- Social, economic, and cultural influences of the healthcare system

Influencing these three components are conscious and unconscious stereotyping and prejudice that can occur with each interaction and may lead to healthcare disparities. Likewise, we have within each of us the power to limit or even eliminate those disparities.

AUTHOR'S NOTE

As a reminder, **cultural sensibility** is a deliberate, proactive behavior by healthcare providers who examine cultural situations through thoughtful reasoning, responsiveness, and discreet (attentive, considerate, and observant) interactions. The healthcare provider is aware of his or her preconceived ideas and biases, but strives to separate personal beliefs from the healthcare provider-patient interaction to provide culturally appropriate healthcare.

Thus far, we have focused on preparing ourselves to be attentive to phenomena that unfold during the patient-provider experience by reconnecting with the essence of healthcare that resides within ourselves (resulting from our original idealism regarding healthcare and our personal motivations/catalysts that led us to this career). We've also identified that at the conscious and unconscious level, all of us have personal BPS.

Before we delve deeper into harnessing our BPS, let's establish a uniform definition for each term (Dictionary.com Unabridged, n.d.):

- **Bias** is a tendency to have partial views toward a subject or person.

- **Prejudice** is a disapproving or negative attitude that is not rooted in fact or accurate information.

- **Stereotype,** according to the sociological definition, is a uniform image that is embraced by a particular group.

Concisely, BPS are manifested as myopic, guarded, and protective behaviors toward a topic or group of individuals. In the following section, we examine the concept of bracketing, which allows us to contain BPS so that they do not inhibit our ability to provide culturally appropriate healthcare.

Bracketing

The word **bracket** (Dictionary.com Unabridged, n.d.) has several definitions, such as a metal or wood joint that provides support; classifying or grouping items; square brackets that are used in writing; and a unit in math that is identified by parentheses. In qualitative research, Husserl's approach to exploring human experiences incorporates bracketing as the first step in a four-step phenomenological process (based on conscious and direct experience) (Hamill & Sinclair, 2010). The process of bracketing is a deliberate and self-reflective activity that involves the researcher identifying at the conscious level all judgments, biases, assumptions, preconceptions, beliefs, experiences, and knowledge the researcher has about the phenomena (human experience) under investigation. Then the researcher consciously gathers his or her preconceptions and suspends them from interfering with exploring the phenomena. Visualize this process as collecting preconceptions into a balloon that is suspended and pulled away into the atmosphere to experience the richness of the phenomena without bias or interference from predetermined opinions. Bracketing in cultural sensibility is a similar process, but not only are the BPS suspended, they are also consciously stopped and prevented from entering culturally appropriate healthcare interactions (see Figure 5.1).

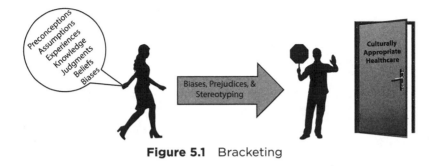

Figure 5.1 Bracketing

Activity: Bracket Your Own BPS

Hamill and Sinclair (2010) provide a sequential process for achieving bracketing in research. Their recommendations will be adapted for our use in bracketing personal BPS as part of cultural sensibility.

1. List personal BPS that you consciously know you possess.

    • Initially, you may draw a mental blank, where nothing comes to mind. Be patient and give yourself permission to write what might not be politically correct. You may only be able to identify one or two BPS.

2. Keep your list handy and pay attention to what you think and privately say about people.

    • This is *your* list. You do not need to share what you write with anyone.

    • Completing this list may take several days, or even weeks.

    • We all have BPS about people.

3. If you're experiencing difficulty creating a list, consider the following questions:

- What television characters irritate you and why?

- Go to your favorite shopping area and document what irritates you about the people you see.

- Consider the characteristics of patients who are difficult for you when providing healthcare interventions. Why are they difficult for you? These individuals may represent a BPS.

4. After you've compiled your list, place each group in a table like the one shown here. Add as many columns as necessary for each BPS identified. Then write under each column comments you've heard or said and any beliefs about the group that reflect BPS toward that group.

Skinny People	Fat People
"They can eat anything they want and never gain a pound." "They're probably anorexic."	"They eat all the time in front of the TV." "They probably don't exercise."

5. Is your comment list complete?

6. Select one group that is closest to a real-life healthcare interaction in your practice setting and complete the following:

- Imagine a healthcare interaction with the group represented.

- Reread the comments you wrote about that group.

- Imagine the healthcare interaction with the group and the comments that were written. (Allow the comments to circle around you and the imaginary individual representing the identified group.)

- Now mentally take all the comments listed for this group and place them in a mega-large balloon. Tie a knot in the balloon and allow the comment-filled balloon to float away from the healthcare interaction with this group. (If you need to, refer back to Figure 5.1.)

7. Using the same group, imagine a healthcare interaction.

8. This time, if any of the comments begin to enter the interaction, stop them by:

    - Recalling that they are suspended in a balloon floating away from the interaction.

    - Referring to Figure 5.1 and stopping the thoughts from entering into a culturally appropriate healthcare interaction. (You are now your own personal enforcer to keep BPS from entering culturally appropriate healthcare interactions.)

    - Stopping the comments by imagining yourself being present in the moment, completely listening to what the individual is saying about his or her healthcare need. (If you need to, create a visual image of ridding any BPS comments from the interaction.)

Congratulations! This is hard work, and you might not be 100% successful the first time you attempt this activity. Like many things in life, the more times you go over this activity, the easier it will become to bracket BPS. The overarching goal is to transfer this mental exercise into our practice setting so that the recognition and bracketing of BPS are almost an automatic response.

9. Repeat Steps 6 through 8 for each of the column groups represented.

In summary, BPS interfere with culturally appropriate healthcare. Bracketing provides a technique for acknowledging and blocking our personal BPS from entering appropriate healthcare interactions. With regard to cultural sensibility, the focus is not on changing BPS but on suspending and blocking them from interfering with the delivery of culturally appropriate healthcare.

Critical Thinking

Human beings have the capacity to think, but few of us realize that there is an art and skill to thinking. The Foundation for Critical Thinking (2013) defines **critical thinking** as an art by which analyzing and evaluating thinking will achieve improved thinking. It further states that a lack of critical thinking can lead to bias, prejudice, or incomplete and hasty thinking that results in poor-quality and expensive decisions to one's self, employment, and society. Critical thinking is a disciplined process that necessitates a self-imposed and cultivated process. The sequential process, as illustrated in Figure 5.2, involves the application of intellectual standards to the elements of thought to cultivate intellectual traits and produce critical thinkers (Figure 5.3).

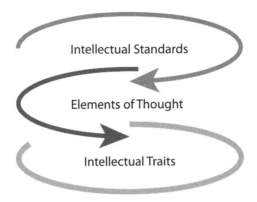

Figure 5.2   Critical Thinking Process

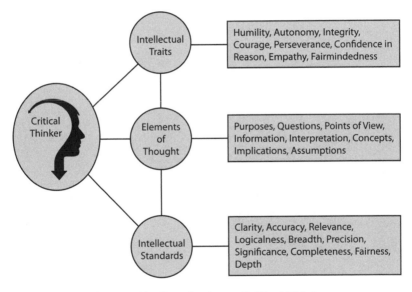

Figure 5.3   Developing a Critical Thinker

The three broad areas that comprise critical thinking are as follows:

- **Intellectual standards** (consisting of the following ten elements):

  Clarity, which seeks additional information on the issue

  Accuracy, verifying the information under consideration

  Precision, seeking additional details

  Relevance, exploring how important the issue is in the broader terms and to other issues

  Depth, delving into the complexities and difficulties of the issue

  Breadth, considering if the issue has been examined from diverse perspectives

  Logicalness, the examination of the process consistent throughout

  Significance, determining whether the issue is the most important aspect to focus on

  Fairness, the issue being presented is without bias and represents diverse opinions

  Completeness

- **Elements of thought** (consisting of the following eight elements):

  Purpose, identifying the goals and objects

  Questions, recognizing the problem or issue

  Information, gathering facts, data, observations, and experiences (Often we stop at experiences and omit the other areas.)

Interpretation, what conclusions and solutions are plausible

Concepts, incorporating theories, definitions, laws, principles, and models into the process

Assumptions, things that might be taken for granted

Implications and consequences regarding the issue

Point of view, developing a reference or perspective on the issue

- **Intellectual traits** (we hope positive, as follows):

  Humility, understanding the limits of your own knowledge and experience

  Courage, being able to deal with viewpoints/opinions you find objectionable

  Empathy, putting yourself in the place of others

  Autonomy, thinking for yourself

  Integrity, being true to your own beliefs and values

  Perseverance, facing up to negative/opposing forces/ideas

  Confidence in reason, trusting rationality to prevail

  Fairmindedness, interacting without a preconceived agenda

For more information about critical thinking, check out the Foundation for Critical Thinking website at http://www.criticalthinking.org. This organization provides numerous free and for-purchase materials on topics relevant to healthcare, including a section titled Nursing and Health Care (http://www.criticalthinking.org/pages/nursing-and-health-care/801). Critical thinking might seem like a monstrous process, especially if this is a new way of thinking. Like building muscles, it requires practice. So, start exercising your critical thinking muscles.

Reflection-in-Action

Reflection-in-action is most notably attributed to Donald Alan Schön (1930–1997), as described in his book *The Reflective Practitioner* (1983). For those who've studied philosophers, you will recognize that Schön's philosophical beliefs embrace John Dewey's (1859–1952) theory of inquiry. Schön believed professionals practiced predominately in a tacit or knowing-in-action categorical context. Knowing-in-action is beneficial, but it can prevent practitioners from recognizing new occurrences (phenomena) that are not related to a practitioner's knowing-in-action categories. However, practitioners who embrace a reflective practice operate from a reflection-in-action perspective in which they are constantly reflecting, challenging, and evaluating their knowing-in-action processes, as well as recognizing, reflecting, challenging, and evaluating new occurrences (phenomena) as they arise (Smith, 2001, 2011).

Applying Schön's reflection-in-action perspective to cultural sensibility, practitioners will need to be in a state of readiness to recognize new occurrences (phenomena) and incorporate these phenomena into and during multicultural interactions. So, to practice cultural sensibility, healthcare providers should practice their respective roles from a reflection-in-action perspective. And with regard to reflection, you can reflect more efficiently if you have the ability and skills to think critically. Therefore, we explored briefly, earlier in this chapter, critical thinking as a precursor to reflection-in-action. An excellent source and the reference for this discussion about critical thinking is the Foundation for Critical Thinking (2013).

Combining the Processes: Critical Thinking and Reflection-in-Action

Critical thinking and reflection-in-action are similar processes. Plymouth University (2010), in its document "Reflection," outlines eight questions students should ask as they try to become reflective learners. The following table includes questions from Plymouth University's "Reflection" and corresponding focus areas that form critical thinking intellectual standards and focus points for each standard.

Steps	Reflection Questions to Ask	Focus	Intellectual Standards	Considerations in Intellectual Standards
1	Who was there?	Descriptive	Clarity, Accuracy, Precision, Relevance	*Clarity*, seeks additional information on the issue
				Accuracy, verifies the information under consideration
				Precision, seeks additional details
				Relevance, explores how important the issue is in broader terms and to other issues
2	What did she say?	Descriptive	Clarity, Accuracy, Precision, Relevance	Refer to above
3	What did I say?	Descriptive	Clarity, Accuracy, Precision, Relevance	Refer to above

Steps	Reflection Questions to Ask	Focus	Intellectual Standards	Considerations in Intellectual Standards
4	Why did I respond in that way?	Analytical/ reflective	Depth	*Depth*, delves into the complexities and difficulties of the issue
5	How did each of us feel as a result?	Analytical/ reflective	Breadth	*Breadth*, considers whether the issue has been examined from diverse perspectives
6	What if I had chosen my words more carefully?	Analytical/ reflective	Breadth	Refer to above
7	So what? Would that have made any difference to the outcome?	Reflective/ evaluative	Logicalness, Significance, Fairness	*Logicalness*, explores if the process is consistent throughout
				Significance, determines whether the issue is the most important aspect to focus on
				Fairness, evaluates whether the issue is being presented without bias and represents diverse opinions
8	Where can I go from here in my interactions with this person?	Reflective/ evaluative	Significance, Fairness, Completeness	Refer to above

The information in this table can help you identify the similarities between reflection and intellectual standards, as well as provide questions and considerations to explore during the reflection process. If reflection-in-action is not already part of your daily routine, developing the habit might require practice. One of the best ways to reflect is to journal. The following activity is designed to reinforce the reflective process.

Activity: Critically Think About a Meaningful Event

According to Branch and Paranjape (2002), reflection-in-action often occurs following a meaningful event. So, in this activity, you identify a recent meaningful event. (Do not select an exceptionally complex event.) After you have identified an event or one part of a larger event, answer the following questions about the event. Don't skip from question to question; answer them sequentially. Remember that you're trying to develop your critical thinking and reflective thinking muscles.

Steps	Reflection Questions to Ask	Your Response
	Overview of the event. • Who was involved in the meaningful event? • What specifically occurred? • How did you respond?	

Steps	Reflection Questions to Ask	Your Response
1, 2, 3	• What additional information is needed about the event? • Is the information you have accurate and verifiable? • What additional details are needed? • How relevant or important is the issue in broader terms and to other issues?	
4	• Why did you respond in the way that you did? • (What are the complexities and difficulties of the issue.)	
5, 6	• Examine the issue from as many diverse perspectives as possible. Think outside of the box. Think about how each person may have felt. • What might have happened if you'd responded differently? Again consider diverse perspectives.	

Steps	Reflection Questions to Ask	Your Response
7	• Now think logically: Would your response have made any difference to the outcome? • Is the aspect that you are focusing on the most important issue of the situation? • Are you examining the issue without bias and considering diverse opinions?	
8	• Evaluate whether the issue is being presented without bias and represents diverse opinions. • What could be your next steps if there is a follow-up to this situation?	

Congratulations! You've just completed a reflective thinking activity.

Now compare your responses with those shown in the table in the "Combining the Processes: Critical Thinking and Reflection-in-Action" section of this chapter. Determine whether you were using both reflective and critical thinking skills. Note that the number of issues, the people involved, the complexity, and the ethical issues in the event you chose to reflect on will influence whether this activity was easy or difficult. (I hope you selected a simple but meaningful event for the activity.)

Activity: Flex Those Reflective Muscles

You review the health history intake for a 35-year-old male who identified his ethnicity as African American, Hispanic, and European American.

1. Describe in writing your initial image of this man. Yes, the first image that came to you as you read the sentence above. Don't worry about what is politically correct. No one will read what you write unless you ask someone to do so.

_____

_____

_____

_____

For many of us, the ability to recognize our mind's picture may be buried so deep in our subconscious that an immediate image might not be recognizable. So, here comes a second opportunity. Do not rush ahead guessing what will be the medical diagnosis or clinical situation.

Now read the following scenario, and then pause and focus on the image that is created in your mind. Ready?

You review the health history intake for a 35-year-old female. She is here today for fertility information and identified her ethnicity as African American, Hispanic, and European American.

2. Describe in writing your initial image of this woman. Remember: Write down the first image that came to mind as you read this scenario.

_____

_____

_____

_____

   I hope this time you were able to recall the image that unfolded.

3. Reread your descriptions for both scenarios.

4. Now recall what you feel about each person you described. Write down your feelings about each description.

_____

_____

_____

_____

The purpose of this activity is not to judge what you visualized or felt. The images and feelings you described are neither right nor wrong. The focus of this activity was on the practice of reflection. Most of us have images, thoughts, and feelings that occur when we experience an initial encounter, but we often ignore them.

As healthcare providers, we try very hard (at the conscious level) to avoid becoming overwhelmed by our multiple roles and tasks. To deal with everything that "is on our plate," we may need to ignore or prioritize images, thoughts, and feelings. If you are assisting with a delicate procedure, calculating a highly toxic intravenous infusion, or responding to an emergency alert, for example, it might be inappropriate to engage in reflection-in-action from a culturally appropriate healthcare perspective. The delicate task is knowing when to address our initial images, when to delay responding to them, and recognizing that they exist.

Now for a few more scenarios to help build critical thinking and reflective thinking muscles.

> You're providing care to a 46-year-old woman who is dirty, smelly, and doesn't speak your language. She arrives at your practice setting out of medications and presents as hypertensive and edematous.

5. Describe in writing your initial thoughts and feelings about this woman.

_____

_____

_____

_____

> You're providing care to a 45-year-old woman who is dirty, smelly, and doesn't speak your language. Roughly every other month, she arrives at your practice setting out of medications and presents as hypertensive and edematous.

6. Describe in writing your initial thoughts and feelings about this woman.

_____

_____

_____

_____

Review your descriptions in Steps 5 and 6. Do any of your descriptions reflect prejudgments or preconceived opinions about people who fit these descriptions? More than likely, the answer is yes. Prejudgments or preconceived opinions are biases, which the majority of us have (and perhaps even embrace in some way). Generally, biases are rooted in our life experiences (our timelines), or they are part of our family norms, values, and beliefs (that is, our culture). Biases can also be rooted in one's social culture (all forms of media, such as print, television, Internet, and so on). Review your responses and try the bracketing techniques previously discussed.

Now review the following descriptions:

> A 35-year-old male identified his ethnicity as African American, Hispanic, and European American.

> A 35-year-old female is here today for fertility information and identified her ethnicity as African American, Hispanic, and European American.

Obviously, I am not there with you to engage in conversation, but I want to generally discuss potential options that may have created the mental image for this man and woman. Respond yes or no to the following questions.

7. For either description, did you visualize either individual in a business suit? If yes, which one?

   Yes ___ No ___

8. Was either individual well groomed? If yes, which one?

   Yes ___ No ___

9. Did you envision them as potential college graduates from Harvard, Yale, or Stanford?

   Yes ___ No ___

The point I am trying to emphasize is that at a very deep subconscious level, we categorize and prejudge. All of us do so on some level or another. It is a part of what makes us wonderfully human. The conflict occurs when we, as healthcare providers, subconsciously or consciously allow our categorizations and prejudgments to interfere with providing optimal, fair, and non-biased healthcare. Perhaps we slip into the job of a healthcare provider instead of *professional* healthcare provider.

The job of a healthcare provider is a list of activities, tasks, and functions. A professional healthcare provider is someone who operates from his or her respective code of ethics/conduct and professional standards and responsibilities and who can separate or bracket his or her personal culture and embrace the professional culture while engaged in professional responsibilities. Most of us slip into the role (mere job) of a healthcare provider at some point during our professional career, but it is important that we support ourselves and each other to retain the energy and engagement to be *professional* healthcare providers.

OPTIONAL WEBSITE EXPLORATION

Project Implicit is a research collaboration that was founded in 1998 to explore unconscious thoughts and feelings on various social topics using association tests. The online Project Implicit is available at https://www.projectimplicit.net/index.html. After reading about the project, select a test of your interest. There should not be a charge for participation with the demonstration tests. Readers visit the website and participate in various tests voluntarily.

AUTHOR'S NOTE

This author is neither affiliated with nor receives any benefits from Project Implicit and is not responsible for negative outcomes from visiting the site. Readers visit the website voluntarily.

Summary

This chapter reminds us that biases, prejudices, and stereotypes abound, even if we're not always consciously aware of them. To provide equitable healthcare, though, we must be professional providers and learn to bracket those potentially negative BPS so that they do not impact the delivery or quality of our care. To successfully bracket them, we must be able to identify them and their influence. Doing so requires both critical thinking skills and reflective skills. The activities in this chapter help us exercise the mental muscles necessary to acquire/enhance those skills.

References

Branch, W. T., & Paranjape, A. (2002). Feedback and reflection: Teaching methods for clinical settings. *Academic Medicine, (77)*12, 1185–1188.

Dictionary.com Unabridged (n.d.). Bias. Retrieved from http://dictionary.reference.com/browse/bias?s=t

Dictionary.com Unabridged (n.d.). Bracket. Retrieved from http://dictionary.reference.com/browse/bracket?s=t

Dictionary.com Unabridged (n.d.). Prejudice. Retrieved from http://dictionary.reference.com/browse/prejudice?s=t

Dictionary.com Unabridged (n.d.). Stereotype. Retrieved from http://dictionary.reference.com/browse/stereotype?s=t

The Disparities Solutions Center, Massachusetts General Hospital (2008). Improving quality & achieving equity: A guide for hospital leaders. Retrieved from http://www2.massgeneral.org/disparitiessolutions/guide.html

Encyclopaedia of Informal Education. Retrieved from http://infed.org/mobi/donald-schon-learning-reflection-change/

The Foundation for Critical Thinking (2013). Retrieved from www.criticalthinking.org

Hamill, C., & Sinclair, H. (2010). Bracketing—Practical consideration in Husserlian phenomenological research. *Nurse Researcher, 17*(2), 16–24.

Paul, R., & Elder, L. (2006). Miniature guide to critical thinking: Concepts and tools. Retrieved from http://www.criticalthinking.org/files/Concepts_Tools.pdf

Plymouth University (2010). "Reflection" learning development. Retrieved from https://www.plymouth.ac.uk/student-life/services/learning-gateway/learning-development

Smedley, B. D., Stith, A. Y., & Nelson, A. R. (Eds.) (2002). Unequal treatment: Confronting racial and ethnic disparities in healthcare. Washington, DC: The National Academies Press.

Smith, M. K. (2001, 2011). Donald Schön: Learning, reflection and change, the encyclopedia of informal education. Retrieved from http://www.infed.org/thinkers/et-schon.htm.

6

YES, WE'RE ALIKE,
BUT THE DIFFERENCES
MATTER

American psychiatrist Abraham Maslow (1908–1970) proposed a hierarchy of needs theory that describes humans as having five basic categories of needs that progress from lower needs to higher needs, as follows:

- Physiological (lowest)

- Safety and security

- Love and belonging

- Self-esteem

- Self-actualization (highest)

Maslow's theory identifies the common, and some might say the universal, needs of mankind. Since Maslow's work in the 1950s, the science community has discovered that humans are 99% or 99.9% (depending on the source) genetically alike, which might explain our similar drives and needs. That remaining 1% or 0.1%, however, results in critical differences that impact biological and psychological differences among and between groups.

1% or 0.1%: Small Difference, Huge Impact

Healthcare providers have known for a long time that some genetic diseases are more prevalent in certain groups than in others (for instance, cystic fibrosis, Marfan syndrome, sickle-cell anemia, Tay-Sachs, and thalassemia). In 2003, scientists identified the 20,000 to 25,000 genes in human DNA as an outcome from the Human Genome Project (1990–2003; http://genomics. energy.gov/). This accomplishment provides opportunities for scientific discoveries and the potential for enhanced deliveries in healthcare.

Ethnopharmacology

Unfortunately, many healthcare providers are unaware of the importance a 1% or 0.1% difference can make in healthcare practice. Documented differences in drug responses among different ethnic groups (and different genetic patterns) have launched a growing specialty called **ethnopharmacology**, where the influence of ethnicity and culture is studied in relationship to the following:

- **Pharmacokinetics:** How the body absorbs, distributes, metabolizes, and excretes drugs (what the body does to the drug)

- **Pharmacodynamics:** Biochemical/physiological effects of drugs on the body (what the drug does to the body)

- **Drug adherence:** Degree to which a patient follows medical advice regarding drugs (dosage, duration, and so on)

- **Education needs:** Dealing with fear, ignorance, myth/superstition regarding drug use/effectiveness

Healthcare providers are encouraged to carefully monitor this emerging field of ethnopharmacology as they seek to improve their level of care for patients from diverse populations. Unfortunately, research in this area is limited and has primarily focused on psychotropic and antihypertensive agents. The following articles, though older, are good primers on ethnopharmacology:

- Ethnopharmacology: The Effect on Patients, Health Care Professionals, and Systems (Warren, 2008)

- Ethnopharmacology: Understanding How Ethnicity Can Affect Drug Response Is Essential to Providing Culturally Competent Care (Munoz & Hilgenberg, 2005)

- Ethnopharmacology (Tripolo, 2005)

- Ethnopharmacology: What Nurses Need to Know (Wessling, 2007)

If you would like to explore this area in greater depth, these are great articles to get you started.

Pharmacogenetics

Though different from ethnopharmacology, as we talk about likenesses and differences, I think it is critical to mention **pharmacogenetics,** "the study of genetic differences in the alleles associated with individual variability in drug response" (Prows & Prows, 2004, p. 63). In short, research is occurring (and some subsequent discoveries) so that drugs can be prescribed based on an individual's genetic test results, instead of the standard prescribing method based on clinical signs and symptoms. Genetic testing (and the resulting pharmacogenetics) is producing hopeful results for some individuals who were once poor responders to broad-spectrum medications. Additional resources include the Cincinnati Children's Genetic Pharmacology Service, the Cincinnati Children's Genetic Education Program for Nurses, and the International Society of Nurses in Genetics (ISONG).

Ethnogeriatrics

The growing population of older people necessitates not only senior-friendly healthcare but also senior-friendly environments that address the needs of ethnogeriatric populations. **Ethnogeriatrics** describes a subspecialty in geriatrics that addresses the diverse ethnicity that exists with elder populations. The American Geriatrics Society, as a special interest group as well as a professional committee, has brought awareness to the specialty of ethnogeriatrics for decades. Today, there are clinical specialties, education programs, and research in the area of ethnogeriatrics.

AUTHOR'S NOTE

According to the Department of Health & Human Services, Administration on Aging (2010), the percentage of individuals 65 years and older in the United States is projected to reach 72 million plus by the year 2030, approximately 19% of the population. Of the 72 million persons 65 and older, 20,758,126 (29%) are projected to be of Hispanic origin.

Yeo (2003) asserts that the healthcare system is ill prepared to manage the projected increase in healthcare needs for elders, because of a lack of sufficient providers. In addition, the system is ill suited to meet the needs of ethnic elders. It is important to recognize that elders enter the healthcare system with lifelong personal experiences; younger providers might overlook their historical longevity and witness to societal events over many decades. Ethnic elders might also be "new" in American society, perhaps after relocating to live with their adult children. If this is the case, they have left behind their cultural roots and now may live in communities without support from their primary ethnic and cultural communities.

In addition, elders who have relocated to the United States might face language barriers for the first time in their life. Imagine that you're an older person who has lived in a community where you were able to speak (and read and write) your birth language and never needed to use English until recently. During your first healthcare visit, in your new community, the provider gives you the following instruction sheet, written in English. To you, the instruction sheet reads like what is shown here:

> *Knaht uoy rof ruoy tisiv yadot. Ruoy noitanimaxe*
> *saw nihtiw lamron stimil. Eht dloob elpmas taht saw*
> *nward deifitnedi hgih loretselohc dna sedirecylgirt.*
> *Ot taert siht noitidnoc evah siht noitpircserp dellif*
> *dna ekat eno telbat htiw tsafkaerb dna rennid.*

How do you feel? What would you do?

Here's the translation:

> Thank you for your visit today. Your examination
> was within normal limits. The blood sample that was
> drawn identified high cholesterol and triglycerides.

To treat this condition, have this prescription filled and take one tablet with breakfast and dinner.

These issues prompted organizations such as the Stanford Geriatric Education Center to investigate, educate, and explore possible solutions to assist ethnogeriatric elders and their healthcare providers in providing culturally appropriate healthcare. One of many techniques to assist providers is the Cohort Historical Analysis Tool (CHAT) (Yeo, Hikoyeda, McBride, Chin, Edmonds, & Hendrix, 1998). The CHAT is designed to assess how historical events in the lives of elders influence their perspective toward systems, specifically healthcare systems. The tool also provides insight into generational diversity.

Why is generational diversity important? Well, consider the following scenario:

> In 1971, PN was 28 years old and lived in South Vietnam fighting alongside the United States against North Vietnam and the Viet Cong troops. After the war, and as a result of Agent Orange, PN watched once lush farmland produce crops that were tainted from the herbicide and numerous men, women, and children develop serious health conditions (tumors, birth defect, cancers, and so on). PN also suffers with painful rashes. As a result of the war and Agent Orange, PN distrusts American science and anything related to the U.S. military. Now 70 years old, PN recently moved to the United States to live with his daughter and son-in-law. PN has a rash outbreak that is severe and looks infected. He reluctantly accepts the urging from his daughter to see a doctor at the nearby government community health clinic. The nurse and physician that see PN are less than 40 years of age and remotely recall that there even was a Vietnam War.

Without assessments related to generational diversity and attitudes toward systems and additional aspects included on the CHAT, healthcare providers will unknowingly encounter barriers during their various interactions, as described in the following section. Even though humans are 99% or 99.9% genetically identical, our 1% or 0.1% differences can have a major impact on healthcare.

Newsflash: Men and Women Differ, Too

As is well documented, men in nursing are treated differently than their female colleagues. Recall Robert, the good-looking male RN you read about in Chapter 3, "Lessening the Impact of Cultural Clashes":

> Robert was in school working toward a master's degree as an advanced practice nurse. He and his fellow students were beginning their initial clinical rotation at the university's multiclinic site. As the faculty member led them on a tour of a particular clinic, the staff began to whisper, and then one said, "Do we get the good-looking male nurse in this group?" "Yes, buddy, it will be a joy to come to work for the next 6 weeks!" "Honey, I will be your personal guide, and we'll make sure you pass."

Had Robert been a female, his colleagues would likely have considered this sexual harassment.

Listed here are some well-known barriers that men in nursing have to overcome:

- They must continually justify their decision to seek a career in nursing rather than medicine.
- They deal with the stereotype that male nurses are gay.

- They are often the only male in their nursing student class and immediate work setting.

- They are often expected to help with the heavy lifting on their assigned unit and to provide care for their assigned patients.

- For many men, socialization is different from how females are socialized. Therefore, male responses in class, clinical, and work settings may differ from women's responses. So, female co-workers may not know how to respond to their male colleagues.

- They might be excluded from certain clinical experiences because of their gender.

- They might not be educated to handle issues and concerns unique to females.

- They suffer continual implicit gender bias from common statements such as the following: "The nurse, she...." "The nurse and her patients...." "Let's recognize everyone with pink...."

- Male contributions to nursing are often omitted from nursing history (Pham, n.d.; Wolfenden, 2011).

Question: If we are more alike than different, why do we allow the previous statements to continually impact our colleagues?

Summary

As you read in this chapter, we're more alike than not, but those small differences (genetic and cultural) can lead to disparate treatment (sometimes negative, sometimes positive). Ethnicity, age, and even gender may sow confusion in the provider-patient interaction if cultural sensibility interactions are not taught, valued, and encouraged. And don't forget that the differences described in this chapter relate just as well to your colleagues in healthcare. Make it your goal to achieve cultural sensibility in all your interactions: with patients, with colleagues, and otherwise throughout your professional and personal life.

References

Department of Health & Human Services Administration on Aging (2010). Chart of population 65 and over by age: 1900 to 2050. Retrieved from http://www.aoa.gov/Aging_Statistics/future_growth/future_growth.aspx

Munoz, C., & Hilgenberg, C. (2005). Ethnopharmacology: Understanding how ethnicity can affect drug response is essential to providing culturally competent care. *American Journal of Nursing, 105*(8), 40–48.

Pham, T., (n.d.). Men in Nursing. Minority Nurse.com. Retrieved from http://www.minoritynurse.com/article/men-nursing

Prows, C. A., & Prows, D. R. (2004). Medication selection by genotype: How genetics is changing drug prescribing and efficacy. *American Journal of Nursing, 104*(5), 60–70.

Tripolo, P. (2005). Ethnopharmacology. *American Journal of Nursing, 105*(11), 48–49.

Warren, B. J. (2008). Ethnopharmacology: The effect on patients, health care professionals and systems. *Urologic Nursing, 28*(4), 292-295.

Wessling, S. (2007). Ethnopharmacology: What nurses need to know. Retrieved from http://www.minoritynurse.com/minority-health-research/ethnopharmacology-what-nurses-need-know

Wolfenden, J. (2011). Men in nursing. *Internet Journal of Allied Health Sciences and Practice*. Retrieved from http://ijahsp.nova.edu/articles/Vol9Num2/pdf/Wolfenden.pdf

Yeo, G. (2003). The ethnogeriatric imperative. *Care Management Journals, 4*(1), 37–45.

Yeo, G., Hikoyeda, N., McBride, M., Chin, S-Y., Edmonds, M., & Hendrix, L. (1998). Cohort analysis as a tool in ethnogeratrics: Historical profiles of elders from eight ethnic populations in the United States. Working Paper 12, 2nd edition. Stanford, CA: Stanford Geriatric Education Center.

7

EPILOGUE

Cultural sensibility is a deliberate proactive behavior we use in both our professional and personal interactions. Remember, too, that cultural sensibility is an ongoing process, as we continue to interact and involve ourselves with others in new relations. Even though an interaction may generate a "déjà vu" experience, every interaction differs. Similarities might exist from one relationship/interaction to another, but they are never exactly the same, if only because of when they occur. In addition, each interaction represents a chance for us to learn something new if we are practicing cultural sensibility. Therefore, by deliberately recognizing and following the process that leads to cultural sensibility interactions, as shown in Figure 7.1, we have the chance to constantly evolve and learn more about ourselves and others. The following section walks you through this process.

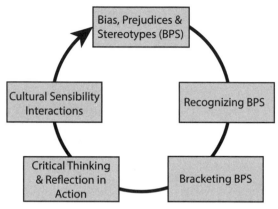

Figure 7.1   Cultural Sensibility Process

Cultural Sensibility: Getting There

As shown in the preceding figure, achieving cultural sensibility interactions involves distinct steps, as follows:

1. **Acknowledge that biases, prejudices, and stereotypes (BPS)** exist in most cultures. As far as we know, BPS are not genetically inherited but are learned and embedded as cultural group values, norms, and behaviors.

2. **Recognize our personal BPS** and how they may interfere with healthcare delivery. In an ideal world, we might try to rid ourselves of BPS, but it could take years to excise BPS that are intricately woven into our personal culture.

3. **Separate personal BPS from the healthcare provider-patient interaction by bracketing our BPS** to provide culturally appropriate healthcare. This is not embracing the behavior of tolerance. *Bracketing* is acknowledging,

clustering, and suspending our BPS from the patient-pro-vider interaction. Once our BPS are bracketed, we can implement the fourth step of the process.

4. **Critical thinking and reflection-in-action** to be fully pres-ent and open to the patient-provider interaction. When these steps are accomplished, we can provide cultural sensibility patient-provider interactions.

The Elephant in the Room

To effectively engage our cultural sensibility, we need to delve deeper into topics we often avoid. "Elephant in the room" is an English idiom that metaphorically recognizes an obvious issue or topic that *should be* addressed but is ignored as if it were not an issue or germane to the discussion (Martin, 2013).

Do you recall the story of "The Emperor's New Clothes"? It's a fairy tale for children, but like most fairy tales, it delivers a lesson. The original story is credited to Prince Juan Manuel of Villena, Spain (1282–1347), but the famous version was retold by Hans Christian Andersen in 1837 (Kurzelil Stories, 2013). The story tells of an emperor who had a passion for, and an overabundance of, clothes. Today, we might say he had a com-pulsion for shopping/new clothes. His every waking moment was consumed with acquiring and flaunting his new clothes. So, the royal tailors were constantly creating something new for the emperor to wear. One day, several scoundrels disguised as tailors arrived at the palace with an offer to make the emperor a new outfit spun from a most powerful and all-knowing cloth. The garment would be visible only to intelligent and worthy subjects of the kingdom. The new garment would be invisible to those in the kingdom who were incompetent, ill prepared, or not worthy to be in the position they held in the emperor's court. The emperor was elated and immediately commissioned the scoundrels to create the new garment. When the imaginary garment was complete and brought before the king, to the king's surprise, he could not see the garment. He immediately became nervous and scared. How could he, as emperor, not be worthy to see the new garment? So, he kept quiet and pretended to see the garment when, in reality, he was dressed in his underwear. Seeing the king's response, his subjects in the royal court began to praise the scoundrel tailors on their workmanship. The king was shocked that his subjects could see the garment but he could not. To maintain his image of being worthy to be king, he commanded a royal parade to showcase his new clothes. The parade began, and everyone knew the king was in his underwear, but no one said a word amidst the cheers of the parade. Suddenly in the crowd, a child yelled, "The king is in his underwear!" Immediately, there was laughter among the crowd as they echoed, "The king is in his underwear."

In this fairy tale, the elephant in the room was that the king did not have on a new outfit visible only to those who were worthy; everyone knew that the king was in his underwear. With regard to cultural sensibility, an elephant may be in the room, but not everyone may even realize the elephant is present. In this final part of the book, we explore a couple of situations when an elephant is in the room but only recognizable to a few individuals (or perhaps just a few individuals are willing to speak up).

But You're Pretty!

Many years ago, I acted as host to a guest of honor during a recognition ceremony. When the ceremony ended, I spent some time with the honoree's family. The conversation shifted to international healthcare. I was asked by a member of the family, who was a young optometrist, if I'd ever been on a medical mission. Smiling, I replied, "Yes." I went on to share that on that particular trip, we might have been the first African-American healthcare team to travel to that particular part of the world. The young optometrist responded by saying, "You're Black? But you're pretty!"

I was not expecting that response. I was shocked, insulted, angry, and violated. I thought of my beautiful biological daughter, my bonus daughter, my sister, my sister-in-law, my mother, my grandmothers, my aunts, my cousins, and my dear "sista" girlfriends. Because I've heard negative comments about the traditional features of African-American women, I believed the optometrist's statement implied the belief that most Black women are ugly. Because my pigmentation has less brown tones, the person may have thought I was White/European American, perhaps suntanned. I thought about responding in a belittling/condescending way, one that would return the favor, insult for insult. In what was probably a nanosecond, those thoughts and so many more raced through my head. Finally, those negative thoughts slowed, and I remembered that my mother raised me better than to lash out. So, I excused myself from the optometrist's presence with, "I'm going to go check on the honoree, excuse me." Other family members of the honoree were standing nearby and overheard this exchange. Their mouths literally dropped open when the optometrist made the comment, but they said nothing.

In this situation, the primary elephant in the room was the optometrist's perception that Black women could not be pretty. I wonder whether the optometrist has ever spent any time considering the personal/cultural BPS. I am sharing this story to highlight how ingrained our BPS might be and also how unintentionally we might expose them (perhaps at the cost of another person's dignity).

After this happened, I told a few people about it. I heard a variety of responses, including the following:

- "Oh, I bet they were joking."

- "You're being too sensitive."

- "They had to have been White."

- "When was that, in the 1960s?"

- "That couldn't have happened."

- "Oh, you must have misunderstood."

- "Surely, they didn't mean what they said."

- "You know it is hard to tell what you are."

- "Well, you know you are light-skinned for a Black woman."

- "I wouldn't have walked away. I would have told them where to go."

Perhaps you agree with some or all of these responses. What I want you to do, though, is to put yourself in my shoes. You feel like you were insulted and disrespected, and you're angry. Then you hear any or all of the preceding responses. How would the original event and then those comments make you feel? I felt like I'd been slapped in the face twice. The following table describes how I perceived these various responses.

Response	How I Perceived the Response
"Oh, I bet they were joking."	Denial and discounting how I felt.
"That couldn't have happened."	
"Surely, they didn't mean what they said."	

Response	How I Perceived the Response
"They had to have been White."	Expressing BPS.
"When was that, in the 1960s?"	The comments are archaic, not really possible now. We've moved on.
"You're being too sensitive."	Blaming me.
"Oh, you must have misunderstood."	
"You know it is hard to tell what you are."	Teasing about my biological make-up.
"Well, you know you are light-skinned for a Black woman."	
"I wouldn't have walked away. I would have told them where to go."	Disagreeing with response choice.

I do not believe that any of the responses were intended to be hurtful or unsupportive. Perhaps some of the responses reflect the respondents' shock at what was said to me. However, no one offered support and comfort during a painful moment. We will never know the intent behind the optometrist's comments. We only have my experience to explore and discuss.

It's *Dr.* Larson to You

Remember Dr. Larson from Chapter 3, "Lessening the Impact of Cultural Clashes"? As you might recall, he was aggressively recruited to serve a rural area with a population of 39,000. He accepted the offer and moved his family to this rural area. A year after moving there, as Dr. Larson was reviewing the physical history of a new patient with gastrointestinal complaints, he asked the patient to describe the color, shape, and general appearance of his bowel movements. The patient paused, looked at Dr. Larson, and then said, "Well, they look like the color of your dark face." Even with a medical degree, Dr. Larson was subjected to racist behavior that left him feeling insulted, disrespected, and betrayed.

Just as in the "you're pretty" scenario, those who hear about this event respond with comments similar to those outlined in the preceding table. We can easily say that the patient, like the optometrist, lacked a filter, mouth control, or political correctness. However, I think that a deeper issue exists here that relates to healthcare education, regardless of discipline. Here's the elephant in the room: We're a multicultural society, but are we really preparing healthcare providers for the good, the uncomfortable, and the hurtful side of multicultural healthcare? Are we preparing healthcare providers for the BPS that they or their colleges may encounter?

Yes, academic professional programs incorporate cultural diversity, cultural humility, culturally appropriate healthcare, the National Standards for Culturally and Linguistically Appropriate Services in Health and Health Care (National CLAS Standards), Joint Commission, and interpretation guidelines. Even so, are we being sensible, culturally sensible, in preparing the Dr. Larsons, Nurse Larsons, Physical Therapist Larsons, and so on to handle situations of this nature? Do their colleagues know how to provide support?

The dearth of healthcare faculty from traditionally under-represented populations in healthcare professional education programs is no secret. So, faculty from traditional majority populations need to deliberately educate themselves about cultural sensibility and become risk-takers to deal appropriately with the very real and very challenging BPS situations that pre-licensure healthcare providers face. I encourage academic programs and healthcare agencies to explore exposing elephants in the room and to create safe spaces for difficult but necessary culturally sensible conversations to occur.

References

Kurzelil Stories (2013). The emperor's new clothes. Retrieved from http://www.kurzweilstories.com/The_Emperors_New_Clothes.pdf

Martin, G. (2013). The meaning and origin of the expression: The elephant in the room. The Phrase Finder. Retrieved from http://www.phrases.org.uk/meanings/elephant-in-the-room.html

INDEX

O–P

Q

R